It's a long road home.

DOUG MCPHILLIPS

Also, by Doug McPhillips:

NOVELS

From Darkness to Light.
Awakened to my Gutted Dream.
The Sword of Discernment.
Santiago Traveller.
I, Prophet.
Master's at my table.
The Guru of Jerusalem.
We are upside down. (Biography)
The Wicklow Way.
The Adventures of Ace McDice.
Instant Karma & Grace.
The Credo.
Reflections of an Old Man.
Reincarnation of the Assassin
Masters of Introspection.
Journey to a hermit's haven.
The Rise and Rise of a 4th Reich
Grandad's tales are tall and true.
Into Action: Alcoholics for Jesus
A Pilgrim's Last Hurrah.
Lightbulb Moments
For Pete's sake
Walking in My Shadow
Sweet Surrender
The Camino Diaries
The Quest: A Santiago Pilgrim's Story.
A Sages Odyssey.

ALBUMS

Country Camino.
Santiago Traveller.
Soul Fact.

Doug McPhillips, Circa 2026, ISBN 978-1-76437270-2-0

National Library of Australia Catalogue-in-Publication data: Holy Bible, International Version, Hodder & Stoughton, 1980. Alcoholics Anonymous, 4th Edition, AA World Service, 1976.
As Bill sees it, 8th Print, AA World Service. 2017
Daily Reflections, 11th Print, AA World Service 2014.
Journey to the Inner Mountain, Hodder & Staughton, 2002.
The Choice is always ours, Jove Publishing, 1997.
The Mythical Journey Simon & Schuster, 1999
The Sword of Discernment, Ingram Spark. Doug McPhillips 2014
Santiago traveller, IngramSpark, Doug McPhillips, 2018.
Lightbulb Moments, IngramSpark, Doug McPhillips, 2025.
Sweet Surrender, IngramSpark, Doug McPhillips, 2026.
The Camino Diaries, Ingram Spark, Doug McPhillips, 2026.
The Quest: A Santiago Pilgrim's Story. IngramSpark, 2026.
A Sages Odyssey. IngramSpark, Doug McPhillips, 2026.

Content.

Introduction.

The email arrived on a quiet afternoon—a formal, polished invitation to participate in an online interview.

The producer’s pitch was highly professional, offering a retrospective on my entire body of work: the songs, the novels, and the overarching theme of personal transformation that defines them. They wanted to explore the anatomy of a spiritual awakening, tracing the line from a past life defined by suffering—a season that brought me to the very brink—to the ongoing creative output that has since become my life’s work.

Thanks to the unpredictable currents of social media, my work has reached a wider audience than I ever anticipated. But prominence is a double-edged sword. In the past, I have tasted my own "fifteen minutes of fame" on two distinct occasions. I know the terrain. I know how easily the ego drinks in the accolades, the kudos, and the superficial validation of the material world. And I know, deeply, that none of it does a single thing for the inner spirit. To live in the logical, linear, first-world matrix is to be constantly tempted by egocentric behaviour. Staying grounded requires relentless, daily contemplation.

So, before responding, I dug deep into the interviewer's background and the agenda behind his employer's mission.

My research revealed a fascinating adversary. The man assigned to interview me was exceptionally well-versed in the art of the celebrity profile, but entirely unaccustomed to someone like myself. He was a creature of pure logic, an archetype of the linear viewpoint, employed by an organisation with its own distinct editorial agenda. He wasn't coming for a spiritual discourse; he was coming to dissect a "victim." I could see the strategy clearly: his questions would be meticulously researched, designed to provoke, strip away defences, and generate engagement without the slightest regard for my feelings or objectivity. He wanted the raw drama of my past suffering, not the quiet grace of the recovery. Yet, despite the potential trap, I found myself drawn to accept.

If I step into this arena, it is not for my own namesake. I care very little about personal branding, except when it can be used as a tool to add credence to a much larger mission. We are living in an increasingly hedonistic world, a society hyper-connected yet profoundly isolated. Every day, I see the fallout: people falling into deep depression, crippled by anxiety, losing confidence in themselves, and, most tragically, losing touch with a God of their own understanding. They have forgotten that spiritual energy is the open secret to existence—the power that allows us to live *in* this world, but remain entirely *not of it.*

The upcoming interview poses a singular, unstated question: *How does a man break completely, yet finish whole?*

The linear, logical world wants a neat, clinical explanation. An audience wants a timeline of events, a dramatic retelling of the suffering, and a tidy bow tied around the scars. But the intellect cannot map the territory of the spirit. A checklist cannot explain a transformation.

To truly answer the questions being posed—not just for the interviewer, but for everyone searching for a way out of the dark—I realised I had to assemble something greater than a simple defence. I had to piece together the fragments of an entire lifetime.

This book is the assembly. It is the connective tissue between the man I was and the mission I now serve. Within these pages, I am pulling the threads from my entire body of work: the novels, which act as hidden maps of personal transformation disguised as fiction; the songs, which captured the raw, emotional frequencies in melody when words alone were not enough to survive the night; and the past life, defined by the cold reality of suffering, superficial fame, and the ultimate surrender that brought me to the brink of a spiritual awakening.

When you lay these pieces side by side, they form a mosaic. They provide a precise, battle-tested answer to the modern crisis of meaning.

I am not writing this to defend my past or to enhance my reputation. I am sharing this collective legacy purely to serve. By examining the wreckage of my linear past and revealing the spiritual energy that carried me through, this book offers a practical blueprint for renewal.

The interviewer might have his agenda, but I have my purpose. Let him ask his questions. The answers are already here, assembled like a mosaic for anyone who has lost confidence in themselves or in the God of their own understanding, and is desperately searching for the way back home.

The interview room is air-conditioned to a sterile, sharp chill. The interviewer is a walking monument to the world I left behind: his hair is cut in a precise, military-grade short back and sides, complemented by a deliberate, one-day-old stubble. He wears a sharp pinstriped suit, a stiff buttoned-up shirt, and a loud, pastel-patterned tie that clashes with the sobriety of his expression. His RM Williams riding boots are polished to a mirror shine, tapping a rhythm of impatient logic against the carpet.

Opposite him, I am a study in deliberate neglect. My beard is unkempt, in desperate need of a trim. I wear a T-shirt of my own design—a simple quill and ink pen bleeding a dark, amorphous blob onto a page—paired with faded, worn-in blue jeans and a pair of blue sneakers, worn comfortably without socks. He is the razor-edged representative of the outer world; I am a traveller, far more concerned with the landscape of the inner one. I pause for the onslaught of questions about what I once was, what changed, and what I am like now.

The Arena of Life on Stage.

The interviewer looked unsettled as he sat before the camera. He leaned forward, his posture rigid, and cleared his throat. He doesn't want the poetry; he wants the anatomy of a failure. And in that fashion, he addressed the studio audience staged for the TV camera:

“Ladies and gentlemen," he begins, his voice dropping into that smooth, practised cadence of professional broadcasting, "we are joined today by Doug McPhillips. A man who has built a prolific, if unconventional, career—a sprawling catalogue of novels, biographies, and albums that claim to chart the hidden geography of human transformation. He presents himself as a guide, a survivor of his own design, and a voice for those lost in the static of the modern age. But beneath the melodies and the prose, there is the recurring shadow of a man who claims to have broken completely only to emerge 'whole.' Today, we are going to move past the myth-making."

He pivots sharply in his chair, the pastel tie catching the light as he fixes his gaze on me, his eyes devoid of anything but analytical curiosity.

"Mr McPhillips," he says, his tone tightening into a clinical sharpness. "Let’s dispense with the stagecraft. You anchor your current identity in the wreckage of your childhood. My question is simple: What were the actual questions that the small, suffering child was asking? What did you believe back then about the dangers of this world, the purpose of your existence, and why you were here?"

The studio hums with a stillness that feels heavy, almost electrified. The interviewer, shifting slightly in his seat, senses the weight of the moment. He reads from his prepared notes, perhaps realising that his "linear narrative" is beginning to fray at the edges, offering a preamble on the necessity of establishing a foundational premise to justify his line of inquiry.

I let him speak. His voice—polished, practised, and rhythmic—washes over me, but it is little more than background static. I am not listening to his words; I am listening to the silence they create. I retreat. I draw my consciousness inward, moving past the velvet chair, past the blinding studio lights, and back into the narrow, shadowed corridors of a house that held a young boy's fears and stifled tears. I am looking for the child who stood in the middle of a world that made no sense, clutching at shadows to find a shape.

"To cast my mind back to my childhood," I begin, my voice sounding gravelly, unrefined, and startlingly real against his broadcast-ready diction. I offer a faint, weary smile, meeting his gaze with a steadiness that seems to catch him off guard. "You must forgive me for taking a moment to answer this. It is a distance I do not travel lightly."

The interviewer pauses, his pen hovering mid-air. He expects a prepared soundbite, but he sees me closing my eyes, anchoring myself in a memory that has no place on a broadcast schedule. In that internal space, the questions return, not as abstract academic inquiries, but as the raw, visceral ache they were when I was small. I ask myself: *Was*

I here by mistake? Why was the air so heavy with the threat of invisible things? If there was a God, why did He allow the walls of my world to feel so thin, so prone to breaking?

I open my eyes, the scene of the studio sharpening once more. I am ready to articulate the bridge between that terrified, questioning child and the man who learned that the "perils" of the world were not the end of the story, but the beginning of the search.

"You ask what I believed back then," I say, leaning forward until the ink-blob on my T-shirt is the only thing standing between us. "You want to know the architecture of my existence. But before I answer, I need to know—are you prepared to hear that the questions I asked as a child were not about *survival*? They were about *purpose*." I wait to see if he will pivot from his script or insist on the tragedy he came here to document.

The interviewer shifts in his seat, the leather creaking slightly under the sudden weight of the shift in tone. His eyes, previously narrowed in analytical assessment, widen just a fraction—the mask of the professional broadcaster slipping, just for a heartbeat, to reveal a flicker of genuine curiosity. He clears his throat, his pastel tie suddenly looking far too bright for the turn the conversation has taken.

"I see," he says, his voice losing some of its clinical cadence. "That's a distinction the audience doesn't often hear. Most would equate early trauma strictly with the fight to survive. You're suggesting that even then, amidst the abandonment and the suffering, there was a drive for something...

architectural. Tell us, then: what was the nature of that 'purpose' you sought, and how did you reconcile that early need to fit into a world that felt so indifferent, with the growing realisation that your path would ultimately lead you inward, through the very suffering you were trying to escape?"

I am aware of the nature of his question, and that he has obviously read some of my books, particularly those on my early childhood. I look at him, then let my gaze wander to the edge of the studio—into the dark space beyond the lights—before bringing it back to rest on the ink-blob on my shirt. The memory is no longer a ghost; it is a weight I have learned how to carry.

"It wasn't that I consciously decided 'this is about purpose' as a child," I begin, my voice steadying. "It was that survival wasn't enough. When you are a child faced with abandonment, you are forced to become a cartographer of your own pain. I lived in a world where the floor felt like it could dissolve at any moment. I found poetry not because I wanted to be a writer, but because I needed a container for the things I couldn't say to the adults who were busy being 'successful' while I was being 'unseen.'"

I lean forward, clasping my hands.

Back then, I spent years trying to figure out how to fit into the world. I studied how other people moved—how they walked, spoke, and the armour they wore—thinking that if I could copy those patterns, the pain would stop. I didn't realise that the suffering was actually a warning. It was a harsh, persistent guide pointing me away from the outside world I was so eager to join, and towards a sanctuary I hadn't yet discovered: the self.

I pause, allowing the truth to hang in the air between us. "I spent most of my life searching for a home through others, in accolades, in the noise of external validation. It took the collapse of all those external structures—the 'breaking' I mentioned in some of my books—to finally realise that the world was never going to give me the answers to what was 'coming down the pike' in my life. The world offers only mirrors; it was only when I finally stopped trying to fit into it and started sitting within myself that I realised the purpose wasn't something to achieve out there. It was something to reveal here." I had touched a hand to my heart. I look at the interviewer, noting the way his pen has stopped moving altogether. "Does that answer the question, or are you still searching for the man who was merely trying to survive?" While the interviewer worked through his prepared questions, occasionally glancing down at his clipboard in search of the next, I retreated into the shadows of my own mind. Once more, I found myself revisiting my early childhood—the loneliness, the abandonment I felt through my mother's inability to nurture me in the way I longed for. I called her "Mother Lode." Even as a young kid, I observed that she possessed a wealth of hidden treasure which she freely shared with others. Yet she seemed unable to nurture her own son.

It was only much later in life that I came to understand that she did love me and cared for me as best she could. What she lacked was not love but empathy, a consequence perhaps of her own depressive nature and the difficult childhood she herself had endured. Manic depression was not a recognised term back then, but by today's understanding, she displayed many of its characteristics.

A flash of memory carried me back to a misty day in May 1950. My brother John, suffering from rheumatic fever, lay confined to his bed. Mother dutifully and constantly attended to him, leaving little of herself for me. I was five years old, and I found relief from my loneliness in my father's company, who, despite his busy entrepreneurial life and the demands of building a business empire, always made time for me.

At lunchtime, we bounded up the back stairs together. John called out from his bedroom as we passed. Mother, who seemed never to leave the kitchen for as long as I could remember, instructed Dad to wash my hands before lunch.
As he was doing so, we heard a scream. We rushed into the room to find John lying back motionless. He was gone. For a brief moment, I relived that childhood pain. I remember then going outside and reinventing myself. Somewhere within that wounded child, I created a new mask, a new identity, one that could survive. That mask accompanied me throughout much of my adult life. So many other tragic events occurred throughout my lifetime, from childhood through my adult years until, through much suffering, I finally broke through the shadow self and became who I am as I am meant to be in the present day. It took further tragedy for creativity to blossom into thirty or so books in my adult years, three

albums of songs, and two decades of writing. Others came to see me as a wordsmith, a creative spirit, perhaps even a sage of sorts. However, that is not how I see myself at all. I am only a fellow traveller who has spent a lifetime searching for meaning among the joys and sorrows of the human journey."

The interviewer, drawing on the connection between childhood trauma, abandonment, and my latter creative life, phrased his question with a hidden sting. "You have spoken openly about childhood trauma and feelings of abandonment that shaped your early years. Looking back now, do you see those experiences as having played a role in awakening your creative expression and your search for deeper meaning?"

I was aware of being pulled into a long discussion I didn't want to have, so I said: "Well, it was through the bridge of many childhood traumas, and the lingering need to hide behind a mask of artificiality, that I was ultimately awakened to the reality of who I had become. Beneath that carefully crafted exterior was a wounded and often forgotten child, carrying the scars of abandonment and emotional pain. Over time, I came to recognise that this hidden child had also discovered a gift. Creativity became a means of survival, a cathartic outlet through which feelings too difficult to voice could find expression in writing and song."

There was no interruption from the very skilled interviewer, so I continued: " What began as a way of coping gradually evolved into a path of self-discovery. Through writing, reflection, and creative expression, I was able to reconnect with parts of myself that had long remained buried. In many ways, my creativity became a bridge between the wounded child I once was and the person I was becoming. The pain itself was never the gift, but it became the catalyst that compelled me to seek healing, authenticity, and a deeper understanding of my own humanity. Through that process, what was once a source of suffering became a source of meaning, not only for myself but, I hope, for others who may recognise aspects of their own journey in my story."

The interviewer believed he had what he wanted to turn the key on his 'victim'. However, he questioned with much charm: "After researching your life, I'm struck by the contrast between the successful businessman you once were and the creative, introspective writer you've become. What prompted this change later in life? Do you think your childhood trauma and feelings of abandonment influenced your shift from seeking external success to pursuing creativity and helping others?"

" I guess I learned to bear a great deal of pain and suffering from an early age. Others followed those first experiences of loss, each leaving its own mark upon my young life. One of the most profound was the loss of my best friend when I was twelve years old. We had gone swimming together in the ocean, and tragically, he drowned. It was an event that remained etched in my memory and one that I later wrote about in my first autobiography. In some ways, I could relate to the themes found in Hermann Hesse's *Beneath the Wheel*, where the vulnerabilities and struggles of youth are portrayed with such honesty and sensitivity. The burdens of childhood are often carried silently, hidden beneath the surface while life continues around us."

I deliberately paused, took a sip of water from the glass provided and continued," Years later, tragedy struck again when I lost my father in a drowning accident. The painful echoes of my childhood loss returned, reinforcing the harsh reality that life can change forever in a single moment. Such experiences do not simply fade away with time. They become part of one's story, shaping perspectives, emotions, and understanding. The grief and trauma weighed heavily upon me throughout my teenage years. At times, it seemed as though I was carrying a burden far greater than my years should have required. Yet, as difficult as those seasons were, they taught me resilience. I learned that while we cannot choose all that happens to us, we can learn how to endure, adapt, and continue moving forward."

Having explored the losses and challenges of my early years, the interviewer shifted his focus to my adult life. He remarked, "You spent many years building a successful business career. That world seems driven more by logic and structure than creativity. Yet business success often demands innovation and vision. What led you down that path, and what later prompted you to swap the boardroom for writing books and composing songs?"

"Every new venture starts with an idea, and every opportunity requires imagination. The search for deeper meaning and purpose did not arise from comfort or contentment. Rather, it emerged from another season of profound suffering in my adult life. By outward appearances, I had achieved what many would regard as success. I had built a successful business, provided well for my family, raised four children, built an investment portfolio, and enjoyed many of the material rewards that self-made business people often aspire to. Yet appearances can be deceptive. Behind the façade of success, life was unravelling. My marriage ended when the mother of my children left me for another man. Around the same period, a close businessman friend took his own life. Then came the greatest blow of all—the loss of my second eldest son, who also died by his own hand.

The divorce was devastating, but nothing compared to the grief of losing my son. I struggled to cope. I turned to alcohol, closed down my business, and withdrew from the world. For a time, I lived almost as a hermit, writing poetry and trying to make sense of the pain. Eventually, after a period in a rehabilitation hospital and much soul-searching, I began to recover. It was from that place of brokenness that a new path emerged—one centred on spiritual growth, creative expression, and the slow process of rebuilding a life with deeper meaning and purpose."

The Lotus Unfolds.

Having listened to the story of success, loss, addiction, recovery, and renewal, the interviewer leaned forward and asked a question that would have me delve more deeply. "How did your spiritual and creative recovery begin, and what led you from the depths of despair to becoming an author, songwriter, and seeker of deeper truths?"

Well, it evolved. The depth of my suffering increased after so much loss and a feeling of loneliness. I retreated into the bush, found a place to live, and partly became a hermit. It wasn't because I wanted to find another way back to reality, but because nothing seemed to work for me. I sought comfort in women instead of God; holding a warm body provided temporary relief, as did alcohol. But over time, these were just passing substitutes for facing myself. Ultimately, I had no choice: I was on the brink of self-harm. I made a conscious decision to give up alcohol, stay away from women, and spend my days walking the bush and along the coastal beaches, in tune with nature—watching birds ride the air currents in the blue yonder, seeing fish return upstream to their source, observing dolphins rounding up fish, whales breaching in the open sea, and even snakes slivering through the grass. The loneliness gave me time to write some in-depth poetry, learn to make clay pottery, and generally take a break to rest and regain some balance in my life. But it wasn't enough.

Gradually, I regained enough strength to return to the city, find a place to live, and begin rebuilding my life. For a while, it seemed as though I was making progress. However, beneath the surface, the wounds remained largely unhealed. It wasn't long before I found myself drinking again, and with alcohol came familiar companions: depression, anxiety, and despair. The temporary peace I had found in solitude began to unravel.

I realised that I could no longer continue as I was; the pain had become too great, and my ability to manage it on my own had reached its limits. Faced with the reality of my situation, I admitted myself to a rehabilitation hospital. What began as an effort to dry out and rest evolved into something far more significant. Stripped of many of my old defences and distractions, I started to confront the deeper causes of my suffering. Looking back, I now see that this was not the end of a difficult chapter in my life, but the beginning of a new one.

The interviewer posed another question: "You often speak about surrender in your books and sometimes in your songs, but when did that journey truly begin for you?

It was a leading question that deserved a factual response: "Honestly, it started whilst I was in rehabilitation, another patient suggested that I should attend Alcoholics Anonymous after I left. It wasn't something I had planned, nor was I particularly enthusiastic about it. But the truth was, I had nowhere else to go."

Before I left rehab, we agreed simply: I would go to AA meetings, but I wouldn't be expected to speak. My only job was to sit, listen, and let the shared stories wash over me. There was no pressure to join in, no need to have answers, and no expectation that I should immediately understand what was being said. So, that's exactly what I did.

I sat quietly in the room and listened. I heard stories of struggle, loss, recovery, hope, and redemption. At first, much of it simply flowed over me, but gradually, something began to change. I started to hear fragments of my own story in others' experiences. These were ordinary folks speaking honestly about their lives, and in that honesty, I found something I had not expected: acceptance. Looking back, those early meetings planted a seed. I didn't walk through the door of AA seeking a spiritual awakening; I went because I had run out of options. Yet in the simple act of listening—without judgment and without obligation—I was introduced to a different way of living. It was there that I first began to understand that surrender was not about giving up. It was about becoming willing to accept guidance from those who had already travelled the road before me.

Of course, I needed to start a new journey in my life. At first, I took part in a series of sharing sessions focused on how to tell your story: what happened, what changed, and what life looks like now. This process made my challenge easier to handle. I began attending these meetings several times a week, sharing my story and learning to surrender to God as I understand Him. I felt I was making progress, though I hadn't yet fully let go and allowed God to enter my life and guide me according to His will. This change happened most unexpectedly during my first walk on the Camino de Santiago. That's when everything started to unfold for me, far beyond what I had initially imagined. I had set out to walk the Camino, guided by the program's steps and daily reflection prayers.

Reflecting on my past, I realise that some form of suffering preceded every significant advancement in my life. Time and again, it was loss, disappointment, struggle, and the humbling acknowledgment of my own limitations—not success, comfort, or certainty—that propelled me forward. What I initially perceived as obstacles often turned out to be the very tools for my growth. It wasn't until much later that I began to understand these experiences were not just random hardships. They were invitations to move beyond my own plans and assumptions toward something greater than myself.

Whenever I stubbornly pursued my own agenda, life found a way to remind me that I was not ultimately in control. However, when I surrendered and became willing to follow God's plan, new opportunities opened up, often in ways I could never have expected. It became increasingly clear that suffering was not the final goal, but rather a catalyst for change. It was how I was shaped, redirected, and prepared for the next stage of my journey. The path ahead was rarely the one I would have chosen for myself, but in hindsight, I can see that each trial carried valuable lessons, and each lesson brought me one step closer to the person God intended for me to become.

My first Camino actually began in Paris. Upon my arrival, I experienced an incident that, at the time, seemed like an unfortunate omen for the journey ahead. While entering the foyer of the hotel where I was staying, I fell face-first onto the floor. Burdened by the weight of my fully loaded backpack, I struck my head heavily, resulting in two black eyes. The following morning, as I travelled by train from Paris to St. Jean Pied de Port, I was nursing a persistent headache from the fall. To distract myself from the discomfort, I opened my diary and began writing. What emerged was a ballad of sorts—a tribute to my grandfather entitled "The Boundary Rider." Once completed, I closed my diary and thought little more about it. It was simply another entry among the many reflections I would record during my pilgrimage across northern Spain.

Some four hundred kilometres later, something unexpected happened. While camping on a mountainside, I made friends with a German rock musician. One evening, he performed a ballad he had written himself. In return, I shared the lyrics of "The Boundary Rider." He was immediately interested and asked for a copy. Over time, he recorded the song on one of his albums. Later, I gave him another poem, and he composed a melody for it, which he included on a subsequent recording. That chance encounter sparked a creative awakening I never expected. Inspired by the experience, I started writing my own songs. Thanks to a fortunate connection with professional musician friends back home, those songs eventually found their way into a recording studio. What followed was the start of a musical journey that continues to this day. I have since recorded three albums featuring both original material and collaborations. Although I was far from skilled on the guitar at first, I gradually learned, and I am now preparing to record yet another collection of songs.

Looking back, I attribute much of my creative growth to a minor incident in a Paris hotel foyer. What initially appeared to be an unfortunate accident turned out to be the catalyst for a series of events that transformed my life. The encouragement I received from a German musician, along with my growing confidence in creating, opened a world of possibilities for me, much like a blooming lotus flower. In the years that followed, this creative energy evolved in various ways. I wrote my first novel, *The Sword of Discernment*, and launched a website, caminoway.com.au, to share information about the Camino, travel preparation, books, music, and other projects. What started as a simple pilgrimage blossomed into a continuous flow of books, songs, reflections, and new ventures.

The whole experience reinforced a lesson that has been recurring throughout my life: events that initially seem unfortunate or painful can later become doorways to unexpected growth. If I hadn’t fallen in Paris, I might never have written "The Boundary Rider." If I hadn’t written that ballad, I may never have met the musician who helped awaken a creative dimension within me. From that single moment, a flourishing of ideas emerged that continues to unfold, changing not only what I do but also how I see myself and the world around me.”

My first Camino was mainly a journey of healing. It helped me let go of much of the suffering, grief, and disappointment that had built up over my life. Through this experience, I learned that the world can be both harsh and kind, and that genuine wisdom lies in learning from both without becoming bitter or naïve. The Camino also stirred a creative part of me that had been asleep for many years. I was inspired to write songs, books, poetry, and start new projects. For a while, I thought that achieving these creative goals was part of my deeper purpose. However, looking back, I realise my ego was still very much involved. Having come close to losing everything, I wanted to leave something behind that would last beyond me.

Two years later, I went back to walking the Portuguese Camino. Along with fresh creative inspiration, I faced a tough relationship that eventually left me emotionally drained. But one big change had happened—I stayed sober. My commitment to sobriety was a major breakthrough in my life. Then, I continued my journey on the French Camino and later took on Ireland's Wicklow Way. These adventures led to more books and songs and gave me plenty of time to reflect. They built my resilience and helped me understand myself better. Still, I eventually realised that neither achievements nor creative work were the real goal. More lessons were ahead, and the deepest insights were yet to come.

The interviewer interrupted the flow of my response with a telling question: "Doug, had the Camino healed you completely, or were there still lessons waiting around the next bend in the road?"

" The honest answer is that I had not yet fully surrendered. While the Camino had healed many wounds, I had not reached that deeper level of trust where I could truly let go and place everything in God's hands. I still felt the need to shape my own destiny rather than fully accept God's plan, or the greater purpose that the Universe might have had in store for me.

I turned to writing in other genres, but I found these imaginary ideas or factual realities unfulfilling. I found myself continually drawn back to the spiritual dimension of life. I came to believe that, sooner or later, every person is confronted by questions of meaning, purpose, and faith. Whether we call it God, the Divine, or simply a higher purpose, there comes a point when we begin to sense that there is a greater plan at work than our own.

For that reason, I returned to writing books of a more spiritual nature. Those were the books that felt most authentic to my own journey and experience. Ultimately, I arrived at a crossroads in my life, but in the interim, those spiritual books served as signposts for others seeking a new direction, hope, or a sense of their own path.

In time, I would discover that neither achievement nor creative output was the true destination. More lessons awaited me, and the deepest insights were still to come."

Recalling my last Camino in 2017, I walked about 1200 kilometres through northern Spain, the Aran Islands, and Ireland before returning home. It was a cold, wet experience for most of the six weeks away. I lived day and night in wet clothes and was suffering from influenza most of the time, along with a severe skin rash that took years to heal. I quit prescription drugs on the route, going cold turkey without medical support. I wouldn't recommend it. Here's the thing: while on the route, having been a sober alcoholic for ten years, I drank one night again. I put this down to the fact that I hadn't attended an AA meeting or read any spiritual literature during my entire time away. I believe the three meetings a week I attended over the ten-year period and the daily ritual of reading spiritual reflections and a work by Bill Wilson, the co-founder, "As Bill Sees It," kept me on track, and during my pilgrimages, I failed to do that. When I got back home, I quickly got back on track and have remained sober ever since.

It is spiritual progress I seek, not perfection, but reflection. This is evident in my writings, which help me cathartically and in turn benefit my readers. Through self-awareness, I gain a new vision in action to overcome the dark, negative side of my nature. It also fosters, dare I say, a kind of humility that makes me dependent on God. Bit by bit, book by book, song by song, I find I can discard the old life—one that did not work in the long run—because in this new life, which works under any daily condition, I can turn to God, set my boat of personality upon the spiritual waters, and go with the flow. All it takes is a tiny touch of the rudder of my existence to stay on course, wherever God may lead.

In doing so, there is no rush to overcome; instead, slow down, write books and songs, and progress in the spiritual life is aligned with divine timing rather than instant gratification. By embracing a slower pace, individuals can overcome the 'hurry disease' of addiction and cultivate meaningful, lasting change.

Writing Between Two Worlds.

The interviewer, seeming a touch frustrated with how this author is steering his story, tries to steer him back to the core of creative work. He shoots a quick question: “When reviewing your body of work—spanning your Camino writings and spiritual reflections to your novels, songs, and poetry—it’s clear that you’re a person searching for something beyond the ordinary aspects of life. Some might even consider you a modern-day hermit or seeker. Are your books an attempt to explain what you have discovered, or are they merely a record of your ongoing quest for meaning? ”

I took a moment to reflect on the question before responding.

"I would say my books are both reflective and narrative. They are also contemplative in nature, both for me, the writer, and for those who choose to read them. I don’t aim to present myself as someone who has reached a final destination of understanding; instead, I write as someone who continues to journey along the path of discovery. Where possible, I seek to illustrate ideas through practical examples. For instance, consider an alcoholic who not only struggles with their addiction but also faces the deeper challenge of surrendering their self-will and placing trust in a power greater than themselves. Recovery often begins when individuals stop trying to control everything according to their own desires and become willing to follow a higher purpose and direction. This principle extends far beyond alcoholism; it reflects a fundamental aspect of the human condition. Each of my books is rooted in a contemplative philosophy that readers may choose to adopt, question, or simply reflect upon. The narrative is carried forward through stories, drawing on my imagination and personal experiences, as well as the wisdom, research, and insights of those who have travelled similar paths before me. Ultimately, my books are not meant to provide all the answers. Rather, they invite readers to engage with the questions and explore their own understanding."

The interviewer nodded thoughtfully before continuing. "Can you provide some practical examples to clarify your points? You've written seven books focused on your experiences walking the Camino, which seem to blend physical travel with inner transformation. You've also extensively explored subjects primarily of a spiritual nature. How do these different works reflect the philosophy you've just described? In what ways do the stories, experiences, and insights contained in them go beyond simple autobiography and serve as practical guides for readers seeking their own sense of meaning, purpose, or spiritual direction?"

“Reflecting on the Camino books now, I realise they emerged during a significant transition in my life, moving from one of the darkest periods into unexpected light. These works were born from a crucible of suffering, grief, and loss. The deaths of loved ones, shattered expectations, emotional turmoil, and the painful lessons learned from confusing lust with love all left their marks on me. The wisdom contained in those books came at a high cost to my health, peace of mind, and, for a while, even my sanity. There were moments when I felt utterly lost, disconnected from myself and the world around me. It was precisely in that darkness that the seeds of transformation were sown. The Camino journeys offered more than mere physical movement across the landscape; they became symbolic journeys through the inner terrain of my soul.

On the surface, the books present travel narratives—stories of pilgrimage and discovery. Beneath the surface, however, they contain deeper reflections on suffering, healing, purpose, and spiritual awakening. Looking back, I can see that they also marked the gradual emergence of my creative imagination as a means of spiritual exploration."

Initially, my understanding of God was mostly traditional. I saw God as the logical, straightforward, historical figure from my upbringing—the one who gave a moral framework and a path to follow. This understanding gave comfort and stability, and it served me well for many years. However, as I kept searching, I began to question and broaden that view.

Gradually, I began to encounter what I can only describe as the God of imagination. This experience was not a rejection of traditional faith but an expansion of it. In moments of contemplation, prayer, writing, and solitude, I discovered a living, creative presence that inspired my thoughts and awakened new possibilities within me. It was as though Christ was no longer just a historical figure to study, but a living reality capable of speaking through intuition, creativity, symbols, and imagination. This discovery profoundly influenced my writing, opening doors I had never considered before. My imagination became not an escape from reality but another way to explore and express spiritual truths. Over time, I came to believe in a God of my own understanding—a God who was both rational and mysterious, historical and timeless, knowable yet ultimately beyond complete comprehension. "

"The God I discovered satisfied both my logical mind and creative spirit. In many ways, it felt like a union between the two halves of my being: the analytical and the imaginative, the intellectual and the intuitive, the historic and the mystical. Once that integration occurred, there was no going back. The books that followed reflected this growth. While my journeys on the Camino remained an important foundation, they gradually became just one part of a much bigger picture. The pilgrimages themselves took up less and less space as my focus shifted to broader spiritual themes and deeper questions about the nature of existence and consciousness."

My writing journey has taken many different forms. Some of my works draw heavily from autobiography and personal experience, while others explore morality through fictional characters and imagined worlds. I have also examined the lives of historical, political, literary, and spiritual figures whose ideas have shaped civilisation and influenced my own thinking. Essentially, each project has been a quest for a deeper understanding of what it means to be human and to live in connection with the Divine. Over time, my writing focus has shifted. What began as stories about personal journeys has evolved into explorations of the spiritual journey itself.

Looking back over the years, I see a common thread running through all my work. Whether I write about pilgrimage, history, imagination, recovery, spirituality, or human character, I am ultimately searching for meaning. Each book marks another step along this journey, another attempt to understand the mysteries of life and the presence of God within it. Most of my current writing reflects this spiritual focus. The outward journey has gradually shifted to an inward one. The landscapes of the soul have replaced the roads of Spain. Yet I have discovered that both journeys lead toward the same destination: a deeper awareness of ourselves, of others, and of the Divine presence that accompanies us every step of the way.

The interviewer, not wanting to be left out of the discussion of his agenda, asked, "Would you highlight some of the main themes that have come up throughout your work and explain why they still hold such significance for you?"

"I would like to answer that question in reverse. The common thread throughout all of my spiritual books is something I did not consciously set out to create. Instead, each book has been an opportunity to explore another mystery of spiritual life as it unfolds before me. I don't approach this with a grand blueprint or a predetermined destination in mind. It often feels as though God is guiding me step by step while keeping the distant horizon hidden from view. I am reminded of the words of Cardinal John Henry Newman, who, during a time of uncertainty and illness at sea, wrote the famous prayer:

" Lead, Kindly Light, amid the encircling gloom, Lead Thou me on. The night is dark, and I am far from home. Lead Thou me on. Keep Thou my feet; I do not ask to see The distant scene; one step is enough for me."

This sentiment has become a guiding principle in both my life and my writing. I rarely know where my journey will ultimately lead. One step is enough, one insight is enough, one book is sufficient until the next one reveals itself. The themes that emerge in my work are not so much planned as they are discovered. In one piece, I may explore tragedy, loss, the collapse of material success, or the courage required to persevere against overwhelming odds. There may be stories of adventure, unexpected changes in direction, and the philosophies that support individuals through life's trials and triumphs. These books often blend fact with fiction, memory with imagination, and reality with symbolism. Like all human stories, they are but a brief wisp of smoke in the greater scheme of things; yet within them lie lessons worth considering. In another book, I may compile the philosophies and observations of famous or infamous figures from history. I am fascinated by what motivated them, what they believed, what missions drove them, and the legacies they left behind. Whether they are saints, poets, politicians, philosophers, or reformers, each life offers insights that can inspire and provoke thought.

“ Some books focus on practical wisdom—the small insights that help us navigate life as it is. These works often explore themes of acceptance, responsibility, resilience, and the understanding that our actions inevitably shape our outcomes. They prioritise actionable guidance over abstract theory, aiming to help people live more effectively and consciously. Others examine the lives of remarkable individuals whose examples can serve as guideposts for those seeking direction.”

"Jesus comes to mind not just as a historical figure but as a living source of wisdom. His teachings continue to illuminate a path towards compassion, forgiveness, humility, and spiritual awakening. Some books encourage readers to plunge into the spiritual waters of life, discovering a freedom that exists beyond fear and limitation. Others delve into themes of myth, sacrifice, suffering, symbolism, and the timeless stories through which humanity has sought to understand itself. I have long been intrigued by how myths and spiritual narratives reveal truths that often transcend reason alone."

" Additionally, there are books centred on introspection—careful observation of one's mental state, emotions, motives, and consciousness. These works encourage readers to explore their inner lives, reflect on their thoughts, and understand the relationship between spirit and personal transformation. Finally, some books draw directly from my own experiences. They consist of collections of memories, reflections, failures, recoveries, and lessons learned along the way. If they serve any purpose, I hope it is to offer encouragement to those who may be struggling through their own nights of the soul."

" If my experiences can inspire others to find hope, courage, or meaning, then the suffering I have endured has not been in vain. Reflecting on these themes, they ultimately lead to the same conclusion. These are books for the progressive soul, centred on growth, transformation, understanding, and awakening. They are written both for the author's benefit and for the reader's, as I, too, am a student of the spiritual life.

The most important theme of all is that none of us ever truly reaches a final destination. We keep learning, stumbling, questioning, discovering, and growing. These books document some of the milestones we encounter along the way."

The interviewer asks, "From what you've said about your books, it seems that the true narrative isn't just about the books themselves, but rather about the personal transformation you experienced while writing them. In hindsight, do you view these works as milestones that reflect a deeper change occurring in your own life?"

"Yes, that is precisely what they were. At the time, I thought I was writing books. Looking back, I realise that God was writing a new chapter in my life. Each book becomes a milestone on my path, documenting where I have been, what I have learned, what I have lost, and who I am gradually becoming. While the writing itself is important, the transformation that occurred behind it is far more important."

The Grace of Surrender.

The interviewer paused for a moment, reflecting on what had just been said. "You have mentioned that your books serve as a record of your ongoing search for meaning and spiritual understanding. However, before you could write those books, something much deeper had to take place within you. It appears there has been a shift from self-reliance, ambition, and the darker aspects of your nature toward humility, surrender, and a willingness to seek God's guidance.

Can you tell us about that transition? How did you move from what you have previously described as the shadowland of alcoholism, fear, and self-will to a life shaped by faith, acceptance, and the practice of letting go and letting God?"

I carefully considered the question before responding.

“The transition I experienced did not happen overnight. In truth, it was the result of years of struggle, self-examination, failure, and, ultimately, grace. The material that led to my books did not come solely from external experiences, but from an inward journey that forced me to confront aspects of myself I would have preferred to ignore. Like all human beings, I have a shadow side—those darker elements of pride, fear, selfishness, resentment, and self-will that had shaped much of my life without my fully understanding their influence.”

“The recovery process through Alcoholics Anonymous (AA) has been one of the most significant turning points in my life. AA taught me that lasting change cannot come from self-reliance alone. For years, I tried to navigate life according to my own plans and desires, only to find myself repeatedly falling into the same destructive patterns. It was only when I became willing to admit my limitations and seek help from a power greater than myself that true transformation began. That willingness was crucial; it opened the door to change. With guidance and daily journaling, prayer, meditation, and honest self-reflection, I gradually prepared myself for change. I began to let go of old ideas and behaviours that no longer served me. The AA literature wisely states, “Some of us have tried to hold on to our old ideas, and the result was nil until we let go absolutely.” Those words held profound meaning for me. To "let go and let God" sounds simple, yet I have found it to be one of the most challenging spiritual disciplines I've encountered. It requires surrendering the illusion that we are in complete control of our lives. It demands trust, patience, and humility. Even today, I continue to learn this lesson.”

“ I have come to believe not only in the existence of God but also in what many in AA refer to as a daily reprieve. My freedom from alcoholism, as well as many of my former undisciplined passions, is not guaranteed by the efforts of yesterday. It depends on maintaining a conscious relationship with God and seeking spiritual progress rather than perfection. Each day begins anew.”

I paused for just a moment to let it all sink in for the interviewer and the audience. “Meditation became an essential part of my journey. In the quiet moments, I found myself more open to a new direction in life. Ideas would surface, insights would blossom, and often, inspiration for future writing would arrive unexpectedly. Rarely did it align with my schedule; more often, it emerged when patience had replaced my striving."

I recall a lesson from an American speaker, John Olson, who shared a powerful message about priorities. He drew a large circle on a whiteboard. He wrote around its edge the various responsibilities that define human life: God, family, friends, work, social obligations, material possessions, and financial concerns. He then posed the question of which should be placed first. Most of us anticipated that he would rank them in order of importance. Instead, he wrote the number one in the centre of the circle and asserted, "They are all number one." His point was both practical and profound. If we spend an entire day focused solely on God while neglecting our other responsibilities, little will be accomplished. Spirituality isn't an escape from life; it is a way of engaging with life. For me, the answer involves starting each day by surrendering myself to God's care and asking that His will be done. Then, I proceed with the tasks before me, trusting that guidance will come when needed. That guidance seldom arrives with dramatic certainty. More often, it manifests as a quiet intuition, a growing conviction, a chance encounter, a line written in a journal, or an unexpected idea that surfaces at the most inconvenient moment.

Yet, reflecting on the years, I can realise that my journey has always been guided. Many of the books I have written are, in one way or another, products of this process. They were born not just from travel, study, or imagination, but from a willingness to seek God's guidance and to follow where that guidance led me. The experiences from my Camino journeys, the spiritual reflections, and the stories themselves all emerged from a life that gradually transitioned from the shadowy realm of self-will into the light of faith, gratitude, and ongoing spiritual growth.

As we deepened our spiritual life, we discovered that awakening to God's grace doesn't eliminate all obstacles from our path. In many ways, it introduces new challenges. We may think that once we surrender our lives to God and seek His guidance, life will become easier and more straightforward, but my experience has often been the opposite. While the path may become clearer, it also demands more from us. Carl Jung understood this well. He believed that genuine transformation requires confronting what he called the Shadow—those hidden aspects of our personality we would prefer to ignore. Recovery, spiritual growth, and self-discovery all require us to venture into these darker regions of the psyche. The old self does not willingly relinquish its authority. Pride, fear, resentment, selfish ambition, and long-established habits resist change, leading us to struggle internally between who we have been and who we are being called to become. Jung referred to this process as individuation, which is the gradual emergence of the authentic self. In spiritual terms, I might describe it as allowing God to shape us into the person He intended us to be all along. However, this process is rarely comfortable. Before new growth can occur, old structures often need to break down. Old beliefs, identities, and attachments may have to be relinquished. What once provided us with certainty may no longer satisfy us, and the familiar world begins to shift beneath our feet.

Sometimes, the people around us find it difficult to understand the changes we undergo. Friends who were comfortable with the person we used to be may become distant. Relationships that once revolved around shared habits, resentments, or ambitions can begin to lose their significance. Even family members may struggle to comprehend the changes happening within us. Although their intentions may be good, they often prefer the person they once knew to the one who is emerging.

At such times, a passage from Scripture comes to mind: Jesus observed that a prophet is seldom accepted in his own hometown. There is profound wisdom in those words. The people closest to us often remember us for who we were—our mistakes, weaknesses, failures, and former identities. When genuine transformation begins, we may find it difficult to reconcile the new person we have become with the old image we held of ourselves. Such a transformation or spirit of awakening can leave us feeling isolated, misunderstood, and even betrayed. There were times in my own journey when I felt very much alone. Some friendships faded, and certain expectations placed upon me by others no longer seemed appropriate. There were occasions when I questioned whether the path I was following was worth the cost. Yet every significant change carries a price. Looking back now, I can see that many of those difficult experiences were necessary. They became the forge in which my character was shaped. The disappointments, losses, misunderstandings, and periods of loneliness were not punishments but rather growth opportunities.

They encouraged me to depend less on others' approval and more on God's guidance. The great spiritual traditions all recognise this truth in various ways. The mystics referred to it as the "night of the soul." The early Christian desert fathers withdrew into solitude to confront their inner struggles. The Buddha left behind the comforts of his former life in search of truth. Throughout history, countless men and women have discovered that genuine transformation often requires a period of uncertainty and inner turmoil. Recovery from alcoholism involves many of these same elements. The alcoholic seeking a new life must abandon more than just alcohol; they must let go of old thought patterns, behaviours, and sometimes entire social circles. This process can feel like a kind of death, but it also marks the beginning of a new birth.

There is a saying found in many spiritual traditions: before we can be filled, we must first be emptied. This observation is very true. Much of my own journey has involved learning what needed to be released before something new could take its place. Pride had to give way to humility. Self-will had to yield to surrender. Certainty had to make room for faith. Control had to be replaced by trust.

None of this happened quickly; it remains an ongoing process. Even now, I continue to discover new layers of myself that require examination and refinement. Spiritual growth is not a destination but a lifelong journey. Once we glimpse a different way of living and experience even a measure of God's grace at work in our lives, it becomes difficult to return to our former existence. We may stumble, feel discouraged, or occasionally lose sight of the path. However, something fundamental has changed within us: we know there is another way.

For me, that understanding became a source of hope. It supported me during times of suffering and despair. It helped me through the long years of recovery, reflection, writing, and spiritual exploration. It inspired the books that came after. Most importantly, it taught me that transformation is possible—not solely through our own strength, but by being willing to place ourselves in the hands of a Power greater than ourselves and trusting that, in time, we will be led exactly where we need to go.

No one escapes the consequences of genuine transformation. When we begin to awaken spiritually, seeking God's guidance and striving to walk a different path, our relationships with the world around us inevitably change. So often leading to a longing for silence over noise, contemplation over constant companionship, and truth over comfortable illusions. As a result, the life we once knew starts to fall away—sometimes gradually and sometimes with startling speed. During this transition, we may find ourselves shunned by those who once embraced us. Friends who seemed loyal may disappear when they no longer benefit from our company or our generosity. We may discover that some relationships were built on convenience rather than genuine affection. Even family members can struggle with the changes they observe within us. Our awakening can, unintentionally, confront them with aspects of their own lives they would rather avoid examining.

What appears to be rejection is often a reflection of their own discomfort, fear, or unwillingness to confront their own responsibilities and inner struggles. This can be a painful lesson, as we naturally seek acceptance from those closest to us. However, spiritual growth sometimes requires us to walk a path that others neither understand nor wish to follow.

In my experience, true transformation occurs when forged in the fire of suffering. Few of us willingly choose the path of isolation, rejection, depression, or despair. Yet, these very experiences often become the tools through which God shapes our character and redirects our lives. There have been times when I felt completely alone, abandoned by circumstances, and misunderstood by those around me. During those dark periods, it seemed impossible to believe that any good could emerge from the pain. However, looking back, I can see that those seasons of suffering were not without purpose. They stripped away many illusions, humbled my pride, and urged me to seek strength beyond myself. What may appear to be destruction at the time can, in reality, be preparation. The old self, with its fears, ambitions, resentments, and attachments, gradually gives way to a new understanding of life and our place within it. In God's perfect timing, we begin to emerge from the darkness with a renewed sense of purpose. We discover gifts and talents that may have been hidden within us all along.

As the years passed, I found myself standing on unfamiliar ground. The person who had entered the darkness was no longer the same person emerging from it. My old identities were fading, and my old ambitions were losing their grip. The wounds that once defined me no longer held that power.

I began to realise that I was entering a new season of life. This was not merely a change of direction; it was a change of being. Though the struggle had shaped me, it would no longer define me. Something new was beginning to emerge, although I could not yet fully see its form. Like Newman's prayer, I was not being shown the distant scene; one step was enough for now.

The books have led me to what lies beyond that threshold, which will become the next part of my journey.

I find myself stepping into a new phase of transformation. The old identities that once defined me are slowly fading into the background. My entrepreneurial drive, the intense pursuit of worldly success, my reliance on alcohol to escape, and my craving for worldly rewards and pleasures—all of these have loosened their grip on my life. While they are not entirely gone, they no longer take centre stage. As I reflect on this transition, I often remember the promises found within the program of Alcoholics Anonymous. These promises once seemed almost unbelievable, but over time, they have become increasingly evident in my own life:

We are told that if we are diligent during this phase of our development, we will be amazed before we are even halfway through this journey and discover a new sense of freedom and happiness. We won't regret our past, nor will we want to shut the door on it. We will come to understand the meaning of 'serenity' and find peace. No matter how far we have fallen, we will see how our experiences can help others. The feeling of uselessness and self-pity will fade away. We will lose interest in selfish pursuits and develop a sense of care for our fellow beings. Self-centeredness will diminish. Our entire attitude and outlook on life will transform. Fear of others and financial insecurity will fade. We will instinctively know how to handle situations that previously baffled us. We will suddenly realise that God is doing for us what we couldn’t do ourselves. Of these, I question the promise of happiness, but I take a leaf out of what Abe Lincoln said: "I am as happy as I make up my mind to be." Besides, I have little time pondering my happiness as I walk the tautly tightrope between shadows and light.

Call to Action.

While I walked the Camino, I experienced what I can only describe as a flourishing of creative inspiration—an ongoing stream of ideas that has benefited others. I deepened my spiritual connection over the past decade. Nevertheless, I felt called to return to the Way of St. James for renewed inspiration and guidance. The Camino has become much more than just a physical journey; it has evolved into a spiritual metaphor for my life.

Tradition tells us that St. James walked and preached a message of devotion, faith, and service. Whether history accurately records every detail is less important than the enduring lesson it imparts. I came to understand that his message can be distilled into a simple principle: actions speak louder than words. This principle resonates deeply with me today. After years of searching, studying, reflecting, writing, and recovering, I increasingly realise that spiritual growth is not measured by what we know, but by how we live. Wisdom that remains confined to books, journals, or private contemplation serves only a limited purpose; it must eventually find expression in action. With this in mind, I see the next stage of my journey reflected in the Twelfth Step of Alcoholics Anonymous.

"Having experienced a spiritual awakening as a result of these steps, we made an effort to carry this message to alcoholics and to practice these principles in all areas of our lives."

For many years, I sought understanding. Then I sought healing, followed by a quest for meaning. Now, I find myself increasingly drawn toward service—not service born of obligation, but service that arises naturally from gratitude. If God has guided me through darkness, addiction, grief, despair, and confusion into a life of greater purpose, then I feel a responsibility to share what I have learned with others who may still be struggling. It doesn't mean preaching or claiming to possess special wisdom. Instead, offering experience, strength, hope, and encouragement are valuable wherever they are needed. It means striving to live according to the principles I have spent many years studying and writing about.

I am reminded of a truth expressed throughout the Christian tradition, particularly by St. Paul: human beings do not exist in isolation. Each of us belongs to something greater than ourselves. We are members of families, communities, fellowships, nations, and ultimately, of humanity itself. We are connected by bonds of love, responsibility, and shared experiences. In a spiritual sense, we are also part of a larger fellowship. Whether we call it the Church, the Brotherhood of Man, the Family of God, or simply the human community, we are called to recognise that our lives are intertwined. Our actions affect others. Our suffering can teach important lessons. Our recovery can serve as an inspiration. Our example can encourage those around us.

This understanding represents a new beginning for me. The years of struggle were necessary. The years of searching were necessary. The books I read were also necessary. However, they were never meant to be the final destination. Instead, they were preparing the way ahead, focusing less on self-discovery and more on self-giving; less on finding answers for myself and more on sharing whatever wisdom has been entrusted to me. In that sense, I feel as though I am once again standing at the start of a journey—not one that stretches across Spain, but a path of service leading into an unknown future. I cannot fully predict where it will lead. However, experience has taught me that I need not see the distant horizon. One step is enough. The next step is enough. For today, that is all that is required.

Whether we call Him God, a Higher Power, or the God of our understanding, we are indeed free men and women. We are neither automatons nor enslaved people. We have been given the gift of free will, and with that gift comes the responsibility to choose how we steward our lives. It is a choice each of us must make. We are called to plan, communicate with one another, live in community, and practice our principles in all our affairs. However, our personal freedom is not unlimited. Freedom without responsibility is simply self-indulgence. We remain servants of God in all that we do and say, seeking, though imperfectly, to align our will with His.

The nature of service can vary greatly from person to person. At times, it may be a humbling experience; at other times, it can be uplifting and inspiring. Service often comes in forms we do not expect or actively seek. However, our responsibility remains unchanged: to respond faithfully to what is placed before us and to account for our lives in alignment with the opportunities and responsibilities given to us. Ultimately, we are not created as isolated individuals. We are meant to live in relationship with one another. We belong to families, communities, fellowships, nations, and, ultimately, the broader human family. Our specific doctrines, denominations, or traditions matter little in comparison to our common calling: to serve God by serving each other. Each of us has a responsibility to contribute to the welfare of our community, to care for those around us, and to be mindful stewards of the world we inhabit. Our gifts and talents are not solely for our own benefit; they are entrusted to us to benefit others in some way.

For me, this service may continue through the fellowship of Alcoholics Anonymous, where I carry a message of hope to those still struggling with alcoholism. It might take the form of writing, social media, podcasts, conversations, or even a simple exchange with a reader like you. Ultimately, the specific form matters less than the spirit in which it is offered. What I have learned is that I do not need to know exactly how God intends to use me. My task is not to control the outcome but to remain willing and available. In His own time, the next step will be revealed, just as previous steps were unveiled when I was ready to take them. I have come to trust in what is often called the slow work of God. Growth rarely follows our timetable. Transformation unfolds gradually, often unnoticed, until we look back and realise how far we've come. Faith requires patience; it asks us to trust the process even when the destination remains unclear. Now, as I stand at this new threshold, I move forward as I have learned to do throughout my life: one step at a time. I trust that the same guiding hand that led me through darkness, suffering, recovery, pilgrimage, and renewal will continue to guide me to wherever I am next called to serve.

I envisage the path that lies ahead of me. Although I may be looking through a glass darkly at this moment, I remain conscious that I am being guided. I occasionally catch glimpses of what might be around the next bend in the road, enough to encourage me to keep moving forward, though never enough to reveal the entire journey. Some insights have already surfaced. For instance, I have considered starting a podcast or hosting a Zoom forum on my website, where readers and fellow seekers can come together to discuss spirituality, recovery, personal growth, and the challenges of living a meaningful life in an increasingly complex world. These ideas do not feel quite ready yet for my books, and songs hold pride of place for me at present, but change is definitely in the air.

The written word can inspire reflection, but personal interaction often brings those reflections to life. Another awakening may represent the next stage of my spiritual development: moving beyond the solitary pursuit of understanding and into a deeper participation in community. For many years, I was content to observe, reflect, and write. However, I increasingly sense a calling to share, encourage, listen, and serve more immediately. If there is a lesson that the Camino, Alcoholics Anonymous, and life itself have taught me, it is that we do not walk alone. We may each travel our own road, but we are strengthened by those who walk alongside us. The wisdom we receive is not meant to be hoarded; it is given so that it may be shared. And so, I find myself once again at a new beginning. The destination remains unclear, but the direction feels right. The years of struggle, loss, recovery, pilgrimage, and writing have brought me to this point. What lies ahead is not merely another ending, but the start of a new chapter; not the completion of a journey, but the commencement of a new phase of service, growth, and discovery. For now, that is enough. One step is sufficient. The next step will reveal itself when the time is right

Reflecting on my writing journey, each book has played a unique role in shaping where I am today. Whether through my narratives about the Camino, my spiritual reflections, autobiographical accounts, or explorations of history, philosophy, and faith, each work has added a new piece to the evolving picture of my life and vocation. The Way of St. James, in particular, offered me much more than a physical pilgrimage. It became a pathway to deeper self-understanding, spiritual growth, fellowship, and ultimately a sense of calling. The lessons I learned on those ancient roads continue to reveal themselves long after the journey has ended. In many ways, I am still walking that.

Through the act of writing, I have often discovered truths that I did not fully recognise when I first put pen to paper. The books became mirrors reflecting my own spiritual progress, doubts, awakenings, and aspirations. That is why I hope my words resonate with others. While our life circumstances may differ, the deeper questions we face remain much the same. We all seek meaning, face suffering, and wrestle with loss, uncertainty, faith, purpose, and the pursuit of belonging. Each of us follows our own spiritual journey. If my writings carry any lasting significance, it's not because they offer answers but because they inspire reflection. They motivate both the author and the reader to continue the journey, to remain open to new insights, and to trust that each step—no matter how uncertain—is part of a greater unfolding. For me, this unfolding persists. The road ahead remains partly hidden, yet the direction feels sufficiently clear. The books have brought me this far, and what lies before me is not merely another writing project; it signifies a new phase of life itself. This phase demands a different expression of the same spiritual principles that have guided me throughout my journey so far.

"It is the outward expression of creativity that has undoubtedly led me to this current transformation." The interviewer interrupted with another question. "I understand what you are saying, but how do you define this transformation?"

I paused for a moment, took a sip of water, and became aware of a familiar encounter with my own consciousness. Unbeknownst to the interviewer, I had...I paused for a moment, took a sip of water, and became aware of a familiar encounter with my own consciousness. Unbeknownst to the interviewer, I had spent much of the previous night wrestling with that very question. Age has brought many gifts, but uninterrupted sleep is not always one of them. Within me remains a certain restlessness—a desire to understand more clearly both the journey I have travelled and the road that still lies ahead.

"Well," I began, "if I approach the question from a dictionary definition, transformation is often described as a profound and fundamental change in the form, nature, appearance, or character of something. That is an accurate enough clinical description. Yet, for the person experiencing it, transformation is rarely neat, orderly, or comfortable. It can be both painful and healing at the same time. It may appear catastrophic as it occurs, only to later reveal itself as necessary. Most often, it is not a single event, but a process unfolding over many years. In my own case, the first stage was loss—deep loss. The loss of family, and in particular, the loss of my son. For others, transformation may begin through the loss of a home, a marriage, a career, or a cherished dream. For me, it felt as though almost everything was stripped away. Family relationships changed, the business I had spent years building disappeared, and the home and lifestyle I had created over decades were gone. Much of what I had regarded as success in life was suddenly at stake."

The Camino helped me let go of the past and opened new channels of creative expression through writing, reflection, and even song. My years of near-hermit existence taught me resilience and self-reliance but also highlighted the importance of solitude as a space for healing. Isolation became less of a prison and more of a workshop for the soul. Time spent in rehabilitation, the benefits of modern medicine, and periods of psychoanalysis all contributed insights of their own. They taught me patience and revealed the slow, often mysterious pace of recovery. Above all, they helped me realise that healing unfolds according to its own timetable, not mine. Writing also became an essential part of my process. For more than fifteen years, it has served as a companion, a teacher, a confessor, and, at times, a lifeline. Through writing, I made sense of experiences that might have otherwise remained fragmented and unresolved. The books became markers along my journey.

What I now see is that transformation is still happening. The difference is that it no longer focuses on what I have lost but on what I am becoming. More and more, I no longer need the rewards the world once offered. Recognition, achievement, possessions, and status matter less than they used to. What matters now is knowing I can still be of service, that I can help others in some small way through what I have learned. But before I can do that effectively, I must keep working on coming to terms with myself. There is still the daily discipline of reflection, prayer, acceptance, and adjustment. I face the challenge of ageing, changing priorities, sleepless nights, physical limitations, and learning to live at a different pace from what once drove me forward. That, too, is part of transformation. For transformation is not just change; it is creation. Each step I take consciously becomes a new act of creation. Every insight I accept, every attachment I give up, and every act of service I perform helps shape the person I am becoming. As I stand on this threshold, I do not see transformation as something that happened to me in the past. It is something that continues to unfold each day. The question is no longer focused on what happened, but on how one lives moving forward.

"Maybe that is the real challenge I face now." I paused again and smiled. "And maybe," I said, "that is where the next chapter starts."

While my past experiences have shaped who I am, so has the childhood conditioning I absorbed from my family, peers, culture, and the education system. For much of my life, I wore a mask built from buried fears, insecurities, and a determination to survive in a competitive world. This mask served its purpose; it helped me navigate life, chase ambitions, build businesses, and seek worldly success. However, it was, in many ways, an artificial existence, driven by external goals and aspirations rather than a true understanding of who I really am. Eventually, that mask cracked.

A Day in the Life.

I spent years climbing a ladder leaning against the wrong wall. It was only when I lost my way, when the material foundations of my life started to crumble, that I was compelled to confront deeper questions of identity, meaning, and purpose. Losing much of what I thought defined me, I uncovered something far more valuable: authenticity. In many ways, my books and songs express this realisation. They are not just creative works; they are attempts to articulate what I have learned along the way. They serve as a form of self-help, not only for others but for myself as well. Each page, chapter, and lyric has helped me make sense of my journey. They are a means to an end, and that end is understanding. So here I stand today. I no longer drink. The fog has lifted, and my vision is clearer than it once was.
The road ahead may be narrow, especially as I approach the later years of my life, but I walk it without fear or favour. It is the path of genuine transformation—imperfect and unfinished, yet real. At the same time, I cannot ignore the wider world around me. We live in an era of extraordinary interdependence, yet one of deep division. Political, social, economic, racial, and ideological conflicts continue to divide people into opposing camps. The threat of war remains. Technology advances at an astonishing pace, yet it often worsens these divisions rather than bridging them.

The world can seem increasingly fragile. In the blink of an eye, much of what we take for granted could be swept away. I cannot ignore the suffering that exists beyond my own circumstances. While I enjoy the abundance available in much of the developed world, countless millions struggle with poverty, hunger, homelessness, illness, and lack of opportunity. Children are deprived of education, and families live amidst violence and instability. Human dignity is often sacrificed to greed, indifference, or the pursuit of power. These realities pose a question that every spiritually minded person must eventually confront.

What is my role in all of this? Am I meant to retreat into a realm of private spirituality, spending my remaining years pursuing personal enlightenment while the world's troubles persist just outside my door? Or am I called to something greater? I don't pretend to have a grand solution. I am only one person. I cannot solve global poverty, end wars, heal political divisions, or rescue humanity from its darker impulses. Yet, I cannot ignore these issues either. What I have come to realise is that world-transforming changes begin with ourselves.

Before we aim to change the world, we first need to undertake the more challenging task of transforming ourselves. We must strive to be more authentic, compassionate, truthful, and willing to serve. The real work starts within us. For me, this means staying present in the moment and attending to the responsibilities of each day. It involves writing, listening, encouraging others, sharing my experiences, and remaining open to God's influence in whatever form it may take. The impact of my contributions may seem small, but consistent, small acts can lead to consequences far greater than we can imagine. Thus, I return to a lesson that has guided me throughout my life: I do not

need to see the entire path ahead; I only need to take the next step.
The transformation continues daily, and the story that unfolds is more about how I choose to live each day than where I am headed.

Turning to the writings of Aldous Huxley is a justification for retreating into myself and stepping back from the world's noise and turmoil. However, I do not view it that way. His words resonate with a truth I have gradually come to accept: before we can genuinely serve others, we must first undertake the challenging task of achieving inner order. There is little value in attempting to heal the world while remaining divided within ourselves. Before I can hope to help another, I must continue the work of understanding my own nature, confronting my shortcomings, and tending to the spiritual responsibilities entrusted to me. Thinking so is not an act of selfish withdrawal; rather, it is preparation. It is the discipline of becoming right-sized by recognising both my limitations and my possibilities. Aside from what I have already written and whatever small service I may still render, I am increasingly drawn toward this inner work, not as an escape from life, but as a means of engaging with it more honestly.

Huxley expressed this beautifully when he wrote:

"The choice is always ours. Therefore, let me choose the longer path—the Promethean way—by carefully nurturing and fueling that inward fire. This small, precious flame, whether kindled or extinguished, shapes the noble or ignoble people we become, the worlds we inhabit, and the very fates that lie before us, our bright or murky stars."

These words resonate with me because they rightfully place responsibility where it belongs. We must first tend to our inward fire. Our character must be cultivated, and our souls nourished. The quality of our outer lives ultimately reflects the state of our inner lives. As I stand at this threshold of transformation, I choose to nurture that inward flame, not just for my own benefit, but in the hope that the light it produces may, however modestly, illuminate the path for another traveller navigating through the darkness. I believe that this is where the next stage of the journey begins."

" My day always begins with a quiet hand over to God —one that I never speak aloud, but that I communicate silently to the morning light, to the God within me, the one I understand in my own way. A prayer less about formality and more about acknowledging the gift of another day and expressing my willingness to be guided through whatever comes my way.

Following this, I engage in the everyday rituals of daily life. I visit the bathroom, wash up, and put on fresh clothes, reminding myself that spiritual living starts not with grand gestures but with simple acts of self-respect and preparation. I then sit down to enjoy a modest breakfast and a cup of coffee while reading a daily reflection from Alcoholics Anonymous literature. These reflections often provide a theme or thought that accompanies me throughout the day. After attending to a few household duties, such as watering the plants and shrubs on my balcony, I head out for a half-hour walk. This walk serves several purposes: it keeps my body moving, clears my mind, and offers opportunities for the usual greetings and exchanges with fellow walkers and neighbours. Something is reassuring about these brief encounters—they remind me that I am part of a wider community, even when much of my work is solitary. Upon returning home, I spend a few minutes stretching to ease the stiffness that seems increasingly determined to accompany me in my later years. I then enjoy a hot shower and change into the clothes that will see me through the rest of the day. More household tasks await. The vacuum cleaner makes its regular appearance, and I attend to various small chores. While these routines may seem mundane, I have come to view them as part of my spiritual discipline. Maintaining order in my surroundings often contributes to a sense of order within my mind.

There isn't much about this life that would capture headlines or inspire admiration. It is simple, structured by routine, reflection, creativity, and service. However, I have come to realise that transformation rarely happens solely through dramatic events. More often, it is found in the consistent practice of small disciplines, day after day, year after year. For now, this is the life I am meant to lead. Tomorrow may bring a new direction or an exciting opportunity. Until then, I will reclaim the power to give and receive love fully, free from the shadows of past hurt, confident that one's heart can remain safer even as it expands. Then, as an afterthought, I add "So I can continue with the routine that sustains me, trusting that in due time, I will be guided to the next right step.

There is another constant I didn't consider until I made spiritual direction a routine part of my daily habits. This constant is the experience of my feelings throughout different aspects of the day. It is a vital part of my needs. While some people, in their spiritual lessons, focus on logical thinking and are more driven by their hearts, I, on the other hand, tend to be more analytical despite my creativity. I need to pay close attention to my feelings to connect with my heart. Old habits die hard, and in the working world, there is often a need to be more logical and less emotional, especially when it comes to running in the cut-and-thrust of business; but it is not so in this spiritual path I follow. It's in the arena of feelings that I navigate by the hour, and sometimes moment to moment, because I need to be in tune with it; it serves me well to keep the head and the heart in balance in all things, whether in the presence of God or in the now.

Feelings are neither right nor wrong; they simply serve as indicators, signposts highlighting aspects of myself that need attention. When I acknowledge them honestly, they often show me where I am resisting life, holding onto old ideas, or where I might be invited to grow. I now view feelings as a bridge between the mind and the heart. The mind offers understanding, structure, and discernment, while the heart brings compassion, connection, humility, and love. Both are essential, and neither is sufficient on its own. My task, then, is not to live exclusively in one realm or the other, but to maintain a balance between them. I aim to think clearly while also feeling deeply, to act wisely while remaining compassionate, and to stay grounded in reality while being open to spiritual movements. It is within this balance that I often sense God's presence and experience the peace that comes from living in the present. It is in the intersection of head and heart that much of my ongoing transformation continues to unfold.

Over time, I have come to understand that feelings are not just emotional reactions to life; they often serve as messengers. If I take the time to sit quietly with my feelings instead of running from them, suppressing them, or rationalising them away, they can reveal something important about my relationship with myself, others, and God. For example, when I experience resentment, I have learned not to immediately focus on the person or situation that seems to have caused it. Instead, I ask myself what part of me has been wounded. Has my pride been hurt? Have my expectations been disappointed? Am I trying to control something that is beyond my control? Similarly, when anxiety arises, I examine the fear that lies beneath the surface. Am I worrying about a future that hasn't yet arrived? Am I doubting God's providence? Am I relying on my own strength instead of trusting the process of life as it unfolds? Even loneliness, a feeling that has accompanied me through many years of isolation and loss, has become a teacher. Initially, I viewed it as something to endure. Later, I discovered that loneliness often holds valuable lessons.

These questions have become as crucial to me as any prayer or meditation. The feelings themselves are neither right nor wrong; they are simply signs—signposts pointing towards parts of myself that need attention. When I recognise them honestly, they often reveal where I am resisting life, clinging to old ideas, or where God might be calling me to grow. In

this way, I see feelings as a bridge between the head and the heart. The mind offers understanding, structure, and discernment; the heart provides compassion, connection, humility, and love. Both are essential, and neither alone is enough. My task, therefore, is not to live only in one realm or the other but to keep a balance between them. I aim to think clearly while feeling deeply, to act wisely while staying compassionate, and to remain grounded in reality while being open to the spirit's movements. It is within that balance that I most often sense God's presence and experience the peace that comes from living in the present moment. There, in the meeting point of head and heart, much of my ongoing transformation continues to unfold.
After many years of seeking meaning through loss, recovery, pilgrimage, writing, and spiritual exploration, I've come to realise that lasting transformation is not achieved through occasional moments of inspiration alone. Instead, it is shaped by the consistent actions of daily life. Morning prayer, taking walks, writing, engaging in conversations, being aware of our feelings, reflecting in the evening, and making a continuous effort to align our will with God's all contribute to the gradual process of growth and becoming.

As the day slowly winds down, I enter an important part of my daily routine. Just as my mornings start with prayer and intention, my evenings often end with reflection. I've learned that if I don't deliberately review my day, much of its worth can be lost. Things happen quickly, conversations fade, feelings come and go, and the next task can overshadow insights. Reflection helps me piece together the moments of the day and look at them more carefully. Usually, I sit quietly

and ask myself a few simple questions: Where did I feel at peace today? Where did I feel troubled? What motivated my actions? Was I acting out of fear or faith? Was I patient when patience was needed? Did I listen carefully to others? Did I try to force my will, or was I open to guidance?
The answers I find within myself are not always flattering. Some days, I notice feelings of impatience, pride, self-centeredness, or a subtle desire to control outcomes. Other days, I experience more gratitude, acceptance, and humility. However, I no longer view these observations as reasons for self-condemnation; instead, I consider them part of my ongoing journey toward self-awareness. Recovery has taught me that progress, not perfection, is the true goal. Spiritual growth follows a similar principle. The purpose of reflection is not to judge oneself harshly but to become increasingly aware of the forces at work within us. I have come to see life itself as a classroom. Every encounter, disappointment, success, irritation, and blessing provides an opportunity to learn something about ourselves. The challenge is not whether lessons are being presented; the challenge is whether we are paying attention.

As I grow older, I've come to realise how vital this awareness is. The ambitions that once drove me have mostly faded. Instead, I now hold a quieter desire to live each day with purpose, authenticity, and gratitude. Some days, I do better than others. There are times when I find myself slipping back into old thought patterns. Still, even those moments are valuable because they remind me that transformation is an ongoing journey, not a finished state. One of the greatest lessons I've learned is that we never truly arrive; we are always becoming. As evening falls and another day ends, I hand over the day's events to God, just as I did with the morning. Whatever I have done well, whatever I have done poorly, and whatever remains unfinished, I surrender it all. Tomorrow will bring another opportunity to begin again.

The realities of aging, occasional sleepless nights, and reflections on what may lie ahead in my later years do not greatly concern me. They are simply part of the process of growing older. Each stage of life brings its own challenges, and old age is no different. At times, I wonder if I will have enough time to complete everything I have started. Books remain unfinished, ideas wait to be explored, and projects sit patiently for my attention. However, I have come to realise that such concerns are largely beyond my control. The truth is, none of us knows how much time we have.

Some days, I find myself slipping back into old patterns of thinking. Yet even those moments have value, as they remind me that transformation is an ongoing process rather than a completed achievement. That is one of the greatest lessons of all: we never truly arrive; we are always in the process of becoming. As evening falls and another day comes to a close, I place the events of the day into God's hands, just as I entrusted the morning unfinished, I surrender it all. I surrender myself to the guidance of the spirits of the past and to God who has brought me this far. Tomorrow, if I am granted it, will take care of itself.

Living the Transformation.

The interviewer, sensing the fear in his interviewee-author, takes the direction and asks: “How can you give unconditional love after all you've been through?”

I had been striving for this for quite some time. Reflecting on all the lost hearts and loves from a fractured past, the answer came with a lump in the throat: “After facing deep hardship and suffering, and forgiving past wounds, my focus now shifts to trusting in the ability to love freely once more. The losses and loneliness have passed; what remains is logical awareness and experience. I recognise that it is possible to offer love and support to others without harming my heart or health. To achieve this, I resolve to set clear boundaries, respect my own needs, and practise self-care. Unconditional love—agape—does not inherently involve suffering. When love flows from a secure and grounded heart, it becomes a source of freedom and wholeness. The true transformation is learning to love openly, wisely, and without fear of loss or damage.’

The interviewer interjects with another leading question. “What template do you use in your experience to achieve the best outcomes of understanding this unconditional love?”

The author responds, but not in the exact direction that the interviewer intended: “ Agape love is not synonymous with suffering. It is a profound freedom—a love that flows from a secure place of wholeness and peace. This shift from pain to trust is the essence of transformation; it is the art of loving with openness, wisdom, and courage.”

The author is sidetracked for a moment, for his mind drifts to an idea to put into action. So it is that these ideas are not expressed to the interviewer but remain in the author's mind alone. A way to put Agape- unconditional love- into the world at large.

He speaks internally: “Having explored the background of my books, my mission to serve others, and the daily practices that nurture my spiritual growth, I am now contemplating what may come next. The tools available to us today are vastly different from those that existed when I first began writing. Although technology presents its fair share of dangers and distractions, it also offers remarkable opportunities to connect, encourage, and support one another in ways we could never have imagined. Increasingly, I consider how these tools can be used to further the principles that have guided my own recovery and transformation.

The idea is still taking shape, and it may evolve into something quite different from what I currently envision. Yet, I can see the potential for an online gathering space—perhaps through Zoom and linked to my website—where readers, seekers, fellow travellers, and those interested in spiritual growth could come together. I do not envision creating another program, a new set of steps, or any attempt to replace the valuable work already done by organisations such as Alcoholics Anonymous. Instead, I imagine an open forum where people can share their experiences, strengths, and hopes.

This gathering would belong not to any one individual, but to the collective wisdom of all participants. Leadership could rotate each week, with one person offering a reflection, posing a question, or introducing a discussion theme. Participants would be encouraged to share their own experiences, insights, struggles, and victories in a spirit of mutual respect and encouragement. The focus would not be on teaching, but on listening. Not on preaching, but on sharing. Not on having all the answers, but on exploring life's deeper questions together. In many ways, this gathering would reflect the principles that have sustained me throughout my own journey: honesty, openness, willingness, self-examination, acceptance, gratitude, and service. Whether this vision will eventually take shape remains to be seen. Like so many aspects of my life, I must leave the outcome in God's hands. My responsibility is to remain open to the possibility and be willing to take whatever next step is revealed.

For now, it remains a seed. Many valuable things start as seeds. In God's good time, it may develop into another opportunity for people to help themselves by helping each other, just as countless others have done before us. If this becomes part of my remaining work, I will gladly embrace it. If not, another door will open. Either way, I have learned to trust the process."

I was sidetracked for a moment, but came back to the line of questioning that the interviewer had asked: "When reflecting on great examples of agape, I find invaluable templates for understanding this profound form of love. For anyone seeking clarity, these exemplars serve as living answers. Consider the compassion of the Buddha, whose life embodied boundless kindness to all beings, transcending personal desire and suffering. Or the sacrifice of Jesus Christ, who offered himself on the cross as an act of ultimate forgiveness and love for humanity, demonstrating selflessness beyond measure. Saint Francis of Assisi, with his humble dedication to poverty and to the care of all creatures, reveals a love rooted in humility and service. In more modern times, Martin Luther King Jr.'s unwavering commitment to civil rights shows agape in action—a fierce, transformative love that seeks justice and dignity for all. And Mother Teresa, who chose to live among the poorest of the poor in Calcutta, exemplifies unconditional love through daily acts of service, bringing compassion without expectation. These luminous lives teach us that agape is not an abstract ideal but a lived reality that changes the world. They inspire renewed courage to embody agape ourselves, guided by the wisdom and strength their lives impart. "

The interviewer leaned forward, as he often did when he sensed there was more beneath the surface to uncover. It was almost as if he had anticipated my thoughts. "Do you believe technology plays a role in spiritual life? "At first glance, this seems far removed from the solitude of your Camino pilgrimages, the quiet reflection that has shaped much of your writing, and the inward journey that defines your search for meaning. Yet, I sense you might be contemplating a new approach to connect with people." Then he followed with a further question: " How do you reconcile the two worlds of the pilgrim's silence and contemplation and the fast-paced realm of technology and digital communication? Are these worlds in opposition to each other, or could they somehow serve a common purpose?”

I took a moment to reflect on the questions before I responded.

"I don't believe technology and spirituality are opposed to each other. The mistake we often make is confusing the tool with its purpose. Technology is simply a tool, much like a book, a printing press, a road, a sailing ship, or a musical instrument. It does not possess moral character on its own; it becomes what we make of it. The real question is not whether technology has a role in spiritual life, but whether we are prepared to use it in a spiritually responsible way. Throughout history, great spiritual teachers have always sought ways to communicate timeless truths. If what flows through us is understanding, compassion, encouragement, fellowship, and hope, then we become instruments of grace. I do not see contemplation and communication as opposing forces; instead, I view them as partners. Contemplation nourishes our inner life, while communication allows us to share it with others. The pilgrim's journey is not complete when he reaches his destination. At some point, he must return home and share what he has learned along the way.

Perhaps that is where I find myself now—Not at the end of a pilgrimage, but at the beginning of a new stage. There is a stage in which the lessons learned along the way are no longer meant solely for my own benefit; instead, they are shared, however imperfectly, for the benefit of others." I paused and smiled. "After all, Agape is not just something we contemplate; it is something we practice."

The interviewer had another question prepared, but we had reached a natural pause. In every meaningful conversation, there comes a moment when further explanation adds little to what has already been said. Words have their limits; beyond those limits lies reflection.

I smiled and leaned back in my chair. "You know," I said, "I think we've explored this topic as much as we need to for today." The interviewer chuckled softly. "You're wrapping up the interview, aren't you?" "Perhaps," I replied. "Or maybe I just recognise that some things are better contemplated than discussed. There comes a point when one must stop talking about the journey and return to actually walking it."

For a few moments, neither of us spoke. The afternoon light shifted in the room. The questions we had discussed—losses, recovery, the Camino, books, the search for meaning, transformation, fellowship, service, and the prospect of new directions—settled into a comfortable silence between us.

"I have learned," I continued, "that life unfolds in seasons. There is a season for striving, a season for suffering, a season for recovery, a season for learning, and perhaps a season for sharing what one has learned. But there is also a season for silence." I paused for a moment. "Much of what has shaped me did not come through argument or analysis; it came through contemplation. It came from sitting quietly with life's questions and waiting patiently for understanding to emerge. The older I become, the less certain I am about many things, and the more comfortable I am with mystery."

The interviewer nodded.

"So, where does the journey go from here?"

I looked out the window for a moment before answering."I honestly do not know, and that no longer troubles me as much as it once did. I spent too many years trying to see around corners that God had no intention of revealing to me. These days, I am content with taking just the next step. One step has always been enough." I gathered my thoughts. "The books have brought me this far. The experiences that inspired them have served their purpose. What lies ahead will reveal itself in due time. My task is not to force the future into being, but to remain willing, attentive, and available when the next door opens."

The interviewer closed his notebook.

"That sounds rather like faith," he concluded.

I smiled.

So it is that this author closes his eyes, gently retreating from the distractions that surround him. In this quiet refuge, he breathes deeply—not with words, but with the pure rhythm of life—each inhale and exhale a prayer unfolding without thought. In this sacred pause, his heart turns softly toward love—the boundless, unconditional love that heals and holds. His breath becomes a silent chant, an offering to the power of agape. With a calm and steady spirit, he opens the door to his inner light and whispers affirmations in the silence of his soul:

"May I love without fear.
May I give with wisdom care.
May my heart be both strong and tender.
May love flow free and transform."

In this moment, pain recedes and trust blooms. There is no rush, no demand—only the profound invitation to rest in the truth that love, its purest form, is both the journey and the destination.

The Correspondence of Courage

Every long road requires a map, and for the world's greatest leaders, those maps were often written in ink on the scrawled margins of history. True transformation has never been a loud, instantaneous explosion; it is a slow, enduring march that begins in the quiet depths of the human soul. Long before they stood before massive crowds or changed the course of nations, figures like Martin Luther King Jr., Nelson Mandela, and Mahatma Gandhi had to navigate their own long roads home—a journey toward inner peace, moral clarity, and the courage to act. They left behind a legacy of deeply personal letters, written from jail cells and exile, that reveal how high philosophy is forged into daily, practical resistance.

The power of these letters lay in their ability to weaponise love and radical compassion in the face of brutal oppression. In 1963, inside a dark, cramped cell in Birmingham, Alabama, Dr. King possessed no desk and no proper stationery. Yet, holding a smuggled, ink-stained scrap of newspaper, he composed a masterpiece of civil rights literature in the margins. He argued that waiting for justice was no longer an option, translating the abstract concept of unconditional love into a tactical blueprint for direct street protest. Similarly, from the isolation of Robben Island, Mandela wrote letters that kept the spirit of an entire movement alive, proving that the pen is a vital companion to the march. These documents were not mere academic exercises; they were strategic directives showing a fractured world how to stand between the oppressor and the oppressed without losing one's humanity.

To survive these long, agonising journeys, these leaders relied on strict daily rituals that transformed their physical actions into living prayers of resistance. For Gandhi, who wrote extensively about *Satyagraha*—or "Soul-Force"—non-violence was an active, fierce commitment rather than passive submission. Every single morning, regardless of political crises or imperial threats, he spent hours spinning cotton on a wooden wheel. This rigorous mindfulness was his armour, protecting his soul from the toxic hatred of his adversaries. Through their correspondence, these mentors shared this essential truth: a person cannot quiet a warring world without first quieting their own mind. In our modern era of deep polarisation, their letters serve as timeless signposts, inviting a new generation to find their own grounding and step forward with a fierce heart and a quiet mind.

A letter from Dr Martin Luther King Jr. was written by him on the corners of an old newspaper- adapted from the spirit of the 1963 " letter from Birmingham jail, written to the clergy and activists at the time.

My Dear Friends,

You wonder how we can continue to walk down these violent streets with smiles on our faces and love in our hearts. You ask me how we can advise our youth to face police dogs and water cannons without lifting a hand in retaliation. The answer lies in a truth older than this nation:

true peace is not merely the absence of tension: it is the presence of justice.

We are caught in an inescapable network of mutuality, tied in a single garment of destiny. Therefore, we do not use

nonviolence out of fear or passivity. We use it because it is the only weapon capable of cutting through hatred without creating more of it. When you look your oppressor in the eye with Agape—unconditional, creative goodwill—you do not surrender. You disarm him. You force him to confront his own conscience. Do not ask when the road will end. Ask yourself what you are doing today to protect the soul of your community. Walk firmly, love radically, and refuse to accept a peace that forces you to compromise your dignity.

In this letter, Dr King dismantles the myth that nonviolence is a weapon of the weak. By invoking *Agape*, he shifts the definition of love from a soft, passive emotion to a fierce, strategic force. For the reader navigating their own long road, King's analysis offers a critical framework: true leadership does not avoid conflict, but uses moral clarity to disarm aggression and demand systemic justice.

Nelson Mandela

The letter is *adapted from his private correspondence to Winnie Mandela and activists during his 27-year imprisonment on Robben Island.*

My Dearest Winnie,

The walls here are thick concrete, and the yard is a grey wasteland of stone and wind. They took my freedom, my name, and my clothes,

reducing me to a number. Yet, as I write these words to you in the dim light of my cell, my entire body throbs with life and is full of expectations. They can confine the body, but no axe is sharp enough to cut the soul of a person who keeps on trying.

To those on the outside who feel weary on this long walk to freedom, tell them this: Patience is not a surrender to time; it is a form of power. Hope is to a freedom fighter what a lifebelt is to a swimmer—it keeps us afloat above the darkest despair. Do not let resentment consume you. Resentment is like drinking poison and hoping it will kill your enemies. We do not fight to replace one master with another. We fight for a society where all people live in harmony. Keep your head

Mandela's reflections from Robben Island redefine the concept of waiting. On a gruelling journey, patience is often mistaken for stagnation, but Mandela frames it as an active form of emotional endurance. By warning against the "poison" of resentment, he shows that guarding one's inner character from bitterness is just as crucial to winning a struggle as outward political resistance.

Mahatma Gandhi, in an adaptation *from his collective essays on Satyagraha and letters sent to his satyagrahis (truth-warriors) during the struggle for Indian independence.*

Friends and Fellow Seekers,

You must completely banish the phrase "passive resistance" from your vocabulary. Passivity belongs to the weak; what we practice is Satyagraha—the pure, unyielding Force of the Soul. It is the total holding onto Truth. It requires far greater courage to stand unarmed before a beating than to wield a sword in anger. If you wish to join this march, your first battlefield is not the British courthouse, but your own heart. You must adapt radically, stand in absolute solidarity with the poorest among us, and commit to a disciplined spiritual practice. When you sit at the spinning wheel each morning, do not view it as a menial task. View it as the quiet tether that anchors your mind. We win over our opponents not by inflicting suffering upon them, but by inviting suffering upon ourselves with patience and sympathy. When the world sees that we are willing to die for the Truth without ever wishing to kill for it, the foundations of injustice will crumble. Fix your mind on the truth, keep your hands busy with service, and the spirit will guide you home.

Though separated by oceans, eras, and distinct political landscapes, King, Mandela, and Gandhi traversed the same moral landscape. *The Correspondence of Courage* demonstrates that their external revolutions were just the outward signs of a deeply rooted inner world. Their letters stand as a lasting proof that true power doesn't belong to those who cause the most pain, but to those who can endure suffering without falling into hatred. King's *Agape* gave the movement its moral strength; Mandela's patient endurance upheld its human dignity; Gandhi's *Satyagraha* powered its unshakeable spiritual drive. Together, they present a unique blueprint for the modern seeker: you cannot heal a broken world with broken tools. To make it through the long journey home, one must hold a fierce dedication to justice, an unwavering inner calm, and the absolute certainty that love remains the ultimate word in human history.

I resonate with St. Paul in his letters to the Romans and Corinthians, in his love for God despite his character flaws, and in embracing the challenge of love.

To the Seekers of the Way,

Do not look upon my ministry and assume I am a man without fracture. I confess to you openly: I do not understand my own actions. For I do not do what I want to do, but the very thing I hate, that I do. The defects of my character are a constant war within my own members. I have begged and pleaded with the Lord to remove this thorn from my flesh, to strip away the weaknesses that make me stumble on this arduous road.

Yet, the answer I received was not an exemption from struggle, but a baptism of grace. I was told, "My grace is sufficient for you, for my power is made perfect in weakness." Therefore, I find the courage to pray through my flaws rather than hide them. I do not wait to become flawless before I step into the dust of service. I lay my brokenness at the altar and press on toward the prize. Let this be my final testament to you as I pour myself out like a drink offering: whatever I do, even in my fractured state, what I do in love, I do for you.

If the letters of history's giants serve as the structural maps for this long road home, it is St. Paul who reminds us that the mapmakers themselves were deeply flawed, beautifully broken human beings. He bridges the gap between the legendary icons of the past and the reality of our own lives. Paul's ultimate surrender—the declaration that everything done in love is done for the Divine—is where the historical

analysis of this book must end, and where the deeply personal must begin.
Because when a traveller acknowledges their flaws, faces their defects, and yet resolves to keep walking, high prose and political manifestos no longer suffice. The journey becomes too intimate for standard text. It requires a melody. It demands a song.

As you turn the page to the final chapter of this book, you leave behind the words of the world's great leaders and step into the raw rhythm of my soul. The songs and poems that follow are my personal messages of courage. They were not written to create a legend, chase profit, or build a grand legacy. Instead, they are the musical footprints of where I have been. Each verse is an anchor: a lesson in the brutal art of letting go, a gentle reminder of the spirit that keeps us grounded, an open hand making amends for past regrets, and a straightforward, honest reflection on the lessons learned along the dirt roads.

This is my final message. It is the expression of a traveller whose deepest wish is to courageously walk that sacred path just one more time—living out every lesson fully, singing every line clearly—before the final surrender to the quiet.

Rhyme and Rhythm.

I now want to share another expression of my journey—my songs. Like my books, these songs did not come from a carefully constructed plan. Instead, they emerged from specific moments along my path, often surfacing unexpectedly as reflections on my experiences, insights, losses, hopes, and spiritual discoveries. Each song represents a milestone along the road I have travelled, serving as a stepping stone in my continuous effort to become a better version of myself and to use my talents in the service of the divine presence within.

For this reason, I have chosen to introduce each song with a brief reflection and interpretation—not to explain its meaning away, but to provide insight into the circumstances and spiritual lessons that inspired it. Just as the books are, the songs are as much a record of my inner journey as an invitation for the listener to reflect on their own experiences. Each song has a specific place in the progression of my life. Some emerged from suffering and loss, while others stemmed from recovery, gratitude, pilgrimage, love, faith, and the search for meaning. Together, they create another pathway through the landscape of the soul.

Before we begin, I want to mention that if you'd like to listen to my songs, you can find them by searching for my name on Spotify or by visiting YouTube and looking up "Top Songs Doug McPhillips," where most of my recordings and albums are available. The first song I want to share with you is inspired by my Camino journey and the lessons I learned about letting go.

It speaks of endings. It speaks of surrender. Releasing our attachments and accepting what is yet to come.

For in many respects, the Camino itself is a lesson in letting go. One leaves behind familiar surroundings, old routines, accumulated possessions and often long-held assumptions about life. The pilgrim discovers that progress is made not by carrying more, but by carrying less.

The same is true about spiritual life. Growth often begins with release. Transformation often begins with surrender,

And so the first song stands as a reflection upon that truth- the necessity of letting go of the past in order to embrace the future that God has prepared for us.

Walking the Camino.

Well, I'm walking the Camino
On The Way to Santiago,
Yeah, I'm leaving here today
'Cause I am on my way,
Walking the Camino,
Walking the Camino.

I'm walking the Camino
On the way to Santiago,
Got a knapsack on my back,
Heading down the track,
Walking the Camino,
Walking the Camino.

Oh! I used to call you honey,
Till you spent all my money,
No use looking back,
just heading down the track,
Walking the Camino,
Walking the Camino.

Well, I had a life of plenty,
Until the pile was empty,
Wine, women and song,
The pleasures are all gone,
So I'm walking the Camino,
Walking the Camino.

Walking the Camino,
On The Way to Santiago,
Got a knapsack on my back,
Heading down the track,
Walking the Camino,
Walking the Camino.

Walking the Camino,
On the way to Santiago,
Just moving right along,
Singing me this song,
Walking the Camino,
Walking the Camino.

There is a profound irony in the written word, especially when it comes to song. When a lyric is sung aloud, the cadence of the voice, the warmth of the tone, and the performer's resonance in his heart vibrates is a spiritual experience.

The next song was inspired by the specific, atmospheric solitude of Lisbon, following a pilgrimage along the Camino de Santiago. On the road, there is a beautiful, brutal freedom. Nature provides—apples are plentiful, bananas are free, and the earth offers its bittersweet bounty to the traveller. You possess nothing, yet you have a place to rest your head. But physical sustenance cannot fill a spiritual void. The journey reveals a deeper poverty: the poverty of isolation. The narrator walks through the world as a wandering soul, looking into the shadowed windows of the city, passing the ladies of the night, observing the transactional offers of intimacy without ever engaging. It is a vital distinction. The song does not drift into lust; rather, it records the profound discipline of a man who witnesses the earthly substitutes for love but chooses to keep moving in search of the real thing.
To be "just another Jesus" on the road is to carry a crown of thorns made of your own memories. It is to feel the weight of every fading past, to look at a handful of sand, and to wonder if the dream of finding a true spiritual counterpart—a Magdalene who understands the depth of your journey—is just another sad song echoing through the streets of Lisbon.
By putting these words on paper, I invite you to look past the metaphor's provocative nature and see the genuine longing beneath. It is the story of a man navigating the thin line between the holy and the human, searching for paradise

across oceans and cities while seeking peace in his own quiet exile.

Magdalene.

Oh! I've tramped the byways
from St Jean on The Way
followed my star
on the Santiago Way.

Couldn't find love there
So I tramped a new route
trudging the pathway
from old Lisbon Town.

Just another Jesus
On the road again
Looking for Mary Magdalene
Looking for Magdalene.

Apple trees are plenty
You can pick your fill
Bananas are free
to eat by the bushel.

Wild berries grow
on the side of The Way
taste the bitter-sweet
of this lonely byway.

Peaches for the taking
plums picked for free
grapes for your fill
Cane sugar for your tea.

Looking for Mary Magdalene
Looking for Magdalene.

So many windows
that never shed light
dark eyes on The Way
ladies of the night,

She's calling me now
some girl of my dreams
Is it just another sad song
in Lisbon.

Maybe she's in Paris
Could it be London Town
here on this pathway
A handful of sand,

Memories of the past
just fading away
Is it just another sad song
in Lisbon.

Looking for Mary Magdalene
Looking for Magdalene.

Birds are flying high
over there in Havana
Flowers are blooming
somewhere in Oceania,

Is this my crown of thorns
A memory stone on The Way
Or just another sad song
in Lisbon.

On the Camino, I met a remarkable monk. He wore a simple habit and sandals. He carried no knapsack. He travelled entirely without money. His days were spent in deep prayer. He lived only to serve others. This man became a living parable. He mirrored the biblical Good Samaritan. His life deeply reflected the spirit of Mother Teresa's brothers. He emptied himself completely to help strangers along The Way.

His selfless journey stood in stark contrast to the modern world around him. Too often, fellow pilgrims are consumed entirely by their own pace, blisters, and destinations. They pass by the suffering of others, focused only on completing their personal trek. This song is a tribute to that solitary monk. It explores radical devotion while exposing the self-absorbed nature of the modern traveller, challenging us to look up from our own paths and see the needs of those walking beside us.

Santiago Traveller.

There's a story that the Christ man told
of a Pilgrim on his way
from Jerusalem to Jericho
On that fate-filled day.

Fortune wasn't smiling
As he came upon some thieves
They robbed him, and they stabbed him
left him there to bleed.

Now it happened that upon the road
A priest was passing near
He saw the young man lying there
But he just passed him by.

Then came a lawyer of business mind
who had more than he could spend
He likewise ignored that man
And on the road he went.

Then came a man both strong and kind
Who put him on his back
carried him to a nearby inn
just a little way down the track

He shared with him some of his food
Left money for his keep
and told the hotel owner
Get him well, I'll pay upkeep.

The man we call a Samaritan
It's the name of those of a kind
who put others before themselves
the poor, the drunk, the blind.

Now, youth today walk on The Way
to discover their own soul
Whilst those of us towards our end
We're letting go of our load.

Suffice to say along The Way
The poor and the lame just beg
Whilst pilgrims on the Camino
see naught but what's ahead.

Santiago Travellers,
doing their own thing
They're walking the Camino Way
for the freedom it will bring.

There's a man walking the Camino Way
He claims no worldly goods
lives on love for his fellow man
carries his own cross.

By day and night, he helps the poor,
the lame, the blind, the lot
Yes, he is Samaritan
On the Camino Way.

The journey of the Camino ends
in the Cathedral at Santiago
were pilgrims flocking in thousands
in their final letting go.

The bishop in his mitre
praised pilgrims with a prayer
The preaching of the dark side gone
Now that we are free to care.

Outside the Cathedral
The beggars line the doors
pleading for some help
from within the sacred walls.

The symbol of the Camino
is but a scollop shell
its many maps on its back
has many tales to tell.

Oh! When you turn it over
It turns into a hand
the one that remains open
for our fellow man.

Santiago Travellers
doing their own thing
walking the Camino
for the freedom it will bring.

Love. When we speak of love, it is often misunderstood. I have had long-term relationships and called them love affairs, but in fact, they were perhaps only the shadow of love. Even my marital life, whilst seemingly a love affair, proved to be a shadow of love itself. When the mother of my children left me for another, I was shattered. At the time, it seemed the greatest wound to my heart. Yet, on reflection, it was not the deep love I thought I had for her, although four beautiful children came forth from that relationship before it ultimately shattered, too.

In the aftermath, I tried hard to bring love back into my life. There are many myths about marriage, but none truly describe the happy union we long for. Myth, rather than showing real love, merely shows how we would like things to be. The images myths offer describe the archetypal ebbs, flows, and conflicts of human emotions. These predictions set us up for how things are psychologically interpreted in any effort at a genuine relationship.

My search more often than not presented me with the shadow of love, with lust at the core of the search for real meaning. There is no recipe for permanent bliss. So often, my relationships with the opposite sex led me to the blues instead of the bliss. Real happiness in any relationship is a product of effort, consciousness, and, to a great degree, a bit of good luck. This next song expresses the crux of my search, my introspection on the subject, and the hope that love will return to take away the blues. It captures the search, the expectation, and the need for comfort, too.

Love.

Is it the sound I'm hearing in the trees,
Or do I see you in the falling leaves?
Maybe it's the sweetness of the breeze,
the feeling of sand between my toes.

We did our mating in some distant past,
Life was always splendid in the grass,
Now feelings are faded memories
And nothing ever lasts for long.

Is this the woman cradled in my arms
the warmth of her constant charms,
maybe it's the child upon my lap,
that sense of innocence.

Oh! Love,
Come back into my room,
And take away these blues.

Did I see you in the corner of my eye?
the shadow of the bird flying by,
the warmth of the sun upon my face,
maybe now in a fading cloud.

Do I see you in the smiling face,
The parade of the human race,
Maybe it's in some isolation
On some foreign shore.

Did you see me somewhere on the road,
Was it a gentle hand upon my back,
Maybe it's the burden of the load
When I look back.

Oh! Love,
Come back into my room,
and take away these blues.

Are you there with the man in the moon,
Did I see you in a shooting star?
that flash of light, a star-studded scene,
that faded out too soon.

Is it true you were there from the start?
maybe back there in my mother's womb,
Where are you now, my gentle one?
Is it because I am lost and worn?

Oh! Love,
Come back into my room,
and take away these blues.

Yesterday we did cartwheels on high,
laughed a lot until we said goodbye,
and the wheel is still spinning,
hoping you will return again.

We came together, staring into space,
listening to the sound between the chords,
danced our way together in the rain,
Then we just died in tune.

Now I am here out upon the track,
walking with my knapsack on my back,
taking the rough with the smooth,
looking for the love that I once knew.

Oh! Love,
Come back into my room,
and take away these blues.

This is the perfect moment to introduce two songs and verses that resonate deeply with my Camino pilgrimage and the profound sense of letting go. They serve as timely reminders of how often we only make true progress through immense pain and sorrow. These memories are deeply seated within my psyche, and they hold a permanent throne in my heart, anchoring a constant ache that may never truly ease.

The first song relates to the tragic death of my father, who drowned while under the influence of alcohol. He was in a terrible state with drink at the time. Yet, he had a brilliant mind and was an absolute genius in engineering. When he died, it felt as though the strings to my puppet self had been severed, leaving me unable to function. Eventually, like turning a page in a book, I learned how to move on.

The second song addresses my son, who died by his own hand—a loss that cut deeper into my circumstances than I ever thought possible. He was the clay that moulded our family together. With our marriage in tatters and the family breaking up, part of his makeup simply could not cope with that reality, let alone his own demons. Walking the Camino helped me a great deal to heal, allowing me to finally process and carry the deaths of those two men I so deeply loved.

Dad and days are gone.

I saw you stumble
I felt your fall
from that great height
on your… majestic wall.

The mind's eye weeping
What a ghostly tale,
as you went stumbling
down that trail.

Well, I watched you rise
to the world of fame
in some midnight madness
on a lonely plain.

Like you, the light blazed
a bright road for me
it only lead to
to misery.

Though you could not see
The rot set in
t'was when I followed
drinking again.

I followed your footsteps
down the dark lit path
on my way out
It could not last.

"You were my hero
Dear love, good old dad,
a drinking companion
Some good times we had
hut mostly just sadness
for the things left undone,

No more cymbals or chimes
No more beats of the drum."

Like you in the power,
once bitten by wine,
gripped by the grape
stumbling blind,

I found my way out,
through a tormented mind,
A power that answers,
much greater than mine.

So, where is the oil rag?
Where is the grime?
Lost in the rhythm
that rambles to rhyme,

Passed by the footsteps,
in the shadow of time,
The engineer drowned
In a fog of wine.

Well, I watch you rise,
To a world of fame,
In some midnight madness,
On a lonely plain.

And I am here now,
biding my time,
Yes, I am here now,
biding my time.

" You were my hero,
Dear love, good old dad,
a drinking companion,
Some good time we had,
but mostly just sadness,
For the things left undone.

No more cymbals nor chimes.
No more beats of the drum,

No more beats of the drum.

Peter.

We had a son named Peter.
was the pride of the family,
Somehow, he became the rock,
The knead that held our clay.

Every kingdom needs a jester,
He was ours, t'was plain to see,
He was always up to mischief,
playing jokes on all he'd see.

True at heart, he was a busy boy,
shooting slugs to kill a rat,
riding motorbikes in Round Up,
climbing trees and all of that!

Loved his model train when raining,
liked to watch eagles fly,
heard the sound of pine trees falling,
with gleeful sparkling eyes.

Love to ride his Yamaha,'
with its long black exhaust,
got his kicks with pro linked suspension,
and low handlebars, of course!

He'd speak of chicken cooking,
and the smell of country air,
of the laughter of some people,
and the roses he smelt there.

Love to feed small pigs when snorting,
hear the thump of rabbits' feet,
watched for hours, small birds flying,
climbing trees and cutting wood!

When we moved into the city,
love to play his rugby game,
didn't like the thought of losing,
Took great relish in the fame!

As he grew, he was a dresser,
wearing his Tag Heuer watch,
always dressed in Ralph Lauren,
Nike Air shoe, his brand of course!

He found joy in Christmas paper,
and the lights of the Christmas tree,
loved to give and watch the smiles,
In a gift-giving family.

Just a boy who loved the world,
all that gathered there within,
through the light of his great spirit,
A darkness was creeping in.

So he drove himself in work life
and he climbed the corporate tree,
but not before he set up business,
with the family and me.

When the darkness in his mindset,
began to take hold,
He took a job in West New Guinea,
where he found a pot of gold.

He got jilted by a lover,
falsely diagnosed as ill,
began to doubt the life he lived,
stopped taking depression pills.

It was then the rot set in,
he decide to let go,
So with a noted pen on paper
said goodbye,
And he just packed it in.

Sometimes when I see a bird fly
I can't help but think of him,
walking hand in hand together,
We were both little boys back then.

There's a cockatoo that's flying
in the shadow land of the heart,
across the great Australian landscape,
on the other side of dark.

Yes, its flight is toward the dawning
where it will cry to the sun,
telling all of nature's glory,
of a suicidal son.

Not all that has passed in my life has been wounding and sad. Quite the contrary, for I have recovered from alcoholism, found a God of my own understanding, and learned to love and respect my fellow man. The adventures of my recent years have added a great deal of meaning to my existence.

The next song lyrics serve as a tribute to that search from long ago, which ultimately guided me into this next phase of life. It mirrors the timeless promise found in the 23rd Psalm:

> *"He maketh me lie down in green pastures: he leadeth me beside the still waters. He restoreth my soul."*

Even after walking through the darkest valleys of grief and addiction, I have found a place of restoration and peace.

When I reflect on a song from the first album, '*The Swagman*', I realise something profound. Despite the sad state of my affairs at the time, I was writing a song that functioned like a prophecy. The lyrics I penned so long ago have since come to pass, perfectly mirroring my current attitude toward everything that exists within and around me today. What began as a creative expression in a dark season has transformed into the very reality I now live.

The Swagman.

Give me the life I love
let the old ways wash by me
keep me cool and by an old gum tree
or a fireside hearth to warm me.

Let me bed down in a cave or tent
by a riverside to bathe me
Such is the life for a man like me
hot damper and tea to hail me.

Here's the heart to start anew
whilst the summer lingers
warmed by autumn's leafy fall
steeled by bitter winters.

Give me the life I love
and the wealth before me
wealth I have within my heart
loves my soul companion.

So let the burden fall
where they may
let what will be wash by me
Give me a blue sky above
and a bush track before me.

Loves may come, and loves may go
Friends are my true reason
for I seek the track ahead
with the Southern Cross behind me.

Let me bed down in a cave or tent
by a riverside to bathe me
Such is the life for a man like me
hot damper and tea to hail me.

So let the seasons come and go'
wherever I may wander
warmed by love of friends anew
with no malice to the foe
nor to life' my reason.

Bind me not to springtime swell
nor yield to come by chance
not the power of the chase
just living the Bushmans dance.

So, let the burden fall where it may
let what will be wash by me
Give me a blue sky above
and a bush track before me.

Wealth I seek not, love nor hate,
nor a star to guide me
just a bush track ahead,
With the Southern Cross behind me.

The Deeper Track

When we search for a new way to live, we inevitably begin an investigation into what life is all about. We turn inward. We introspect on our deeper track, seeking the true path we are meant to take.

Eventually, inner reflection demands open observation. We must articulate what we have found. For me, that articulation took form in the melody and truth of this next song: "Wounded Love Heart."

It did not come quickly, as many of my songs have. I was reflecting on how I had spent too long trapped in the city. I was confined to a pent-up room, feeling the weight of that quiet desperation. After a long absence, I finally began the long journey home. It was during that transit—as the city faded behind me—that my pen found its release. I realised I had to step to my own music. In that awakening, the song was born.

Wounded love heart.

Now my heart beats
to a drummer,
That's not quite the same as the rest,
It's where I long to be free,
attuned with the sound in my chest.

Listen to the rhythm of a heartbeat,
The sound of a different drum,
not the beat of a heart for another,
nor the weary heart wounded by love.

It won't be found in worldly values,
where money's the ultimate quest,
not the beat of a heart in battle,
where they pin a medal on your breast.

It may be found when in tune with nature,
where man is at one with the plan,
climbing a rugged mountain range,
tilling and planting the land.

Sailing the blue of the ocean,
viewing the flight of a bird,
hearing the sound of cicadas,
deep in a forested wood.

Catching a fish for survival,
cooking it on one's fire,
sleeping out in the open,
Watching the star-filled sky.

Seeing the sunrise at dawn,
plainly being in tune,
living the now when it's crowded,
being quite still in a room.

It's being in tune with one's senses,
The music you have in your heart,
conscious of each passing moment,
The wounded love hearts are where you start.

It won't be found in worldly values,
where money is the ultimate quest,
not the beat of a heart in battle,
where they pinned a medal on your breast.

Now I know my heart beats
to a drummer,
That's not quite the same as the rest,
It's where I long to be free,
attuned with the sound in my chest.

The old man at the sidewalk cafe is a reflection on the later years of life and the questions that often accompany retirement. Having left behind the demands and routines of a working life, the old man finds himself sitting alone at a sidewalk café, watching the endless stream of people hurrying by. He observes the restless energy of the crowd as they pursue their ambitions, obligations, and desires, caught up in the race of everyday life.

As he sits and reflects, he becomes aware of the passage of time. The tolling of a distant bell reminds him of his own mortality, and he wonders if the next call may one day be for him. In that quiet moment, he weighs the value of a life spent striving against the wisdom that comes from stepping aside and observing.

Yet beneath his contemplation lies another question: Has his work in the world truly come to an end, or does he still have one more contribution to make? The piece explores the tension between acceptance and ambition, between a peaceful retirement and the desire to re-enter the arena of life. It serves as a meditation on purpose, aging, and the search for meaning as one approaches the final chapters of life's journey.

Old man at the sidewalk cafe.

There's an old man
at the sidewalk cafe
drinking his coffee slowly
sitting there taking it easy
no longer on the go.

Is that the old man
who made a fortune
The hero of Big Dome and Co?
Didn't he see it crumble
or did he just let it go?

Does that old man know the wisdom
sitting there taking it slow
watching the passing parade
learning to live and let go.

Oh! He knows his time is fading
the sunsets kicking in
He can hear the bell tolling
Is it ringing just for him?

See the old man
at the sidewalk cafe
drinking his coffee neat
lost in a dream of past glory
fading so slowly with him.

Does that old man know the wisdom
sitting there taking it slow
watching the passing parade
learning to live and let go.

Is that the same old man
at the sidewalk cafe
doing the best that he can
learning to live, to love and let go
Maybe starting all over again?

Does he think it's not too late
The game of patience, the go
waiting for the hand of fate
drinking his coffee neat
sitting there taking it slow.

Does that old man know the wisdom
sitting there taking it slow
watching the passing parade
learning to love and let go.

I could continue to reflect on growing older, the stories behind my books, and the legacy I might one day leave behind. However, I have learned to be cautious about taking myself too seriously or placing excessive value on my own words. There can be an egocentricity that quietly accompanies such reflections, a trait I no longer seek, although I recognise that traces of it still linger.

The ego, after all, is akin to a grain of sand on a vast beach. It has its place but must remain just that—a grain of sand—and not be allowed to consume the entire beach.

The next song echoes this understanding. It recalls a distant walk I once took through the Pyrenees Mountains, a journey I undertook in search of solitude, freedom, and inner peace. In a reflective and somewhat melancholic state, I find myself remembering that time and place. Among those memories is the fleeting image of a woman who appeared in my thoughts and imaginings. Whether she represented a real person, a longing of the heart, or simply a distraction along the path, I cannot say for certain. Yet her presence serves as a reminder that even when we seek peace and spiritual clarity, yet the attractions and desires of the world continue to accompany us.

As I reflect on that journey, I realise that if I were ever to return, it wouldn't be in pursuit of worldly ambitions, romantic fantasies, or personal achievements. Instead, it would be for the freedom of the spirit, the simplicity of being, and the quiet communion found when one steps away from the noise of the world and walks alone with one's thoughts. In this way, the mountains symbolise not just a destination but the inner journey itself. It is a good note to finish the book on.

The Mountains of the Pyrenees.

Now I've been called a legend,
Wordsmith of books and songs,
But worlds don’t express my feelings
And they sure don't keep me warm.

These days, I claim no title,
Nor do I seek any raise,
For words are just expressions
They are not hearts’ love to praise.

Oh! The sun casts shadows on my wall,
There’s a prayer on every stone and tree,
I hear the cock crow a reminder,
The mountains of the Pyrenees.

Now my heart is lost in dreaming,
Wishing you were back with me,
Putting aside pain and sorrow
Calling me back to the Pyrenees.

When we parted with sweet sorrow,
Remembering the way we were,
The call to be a rover there
The Mountains of the Pyrenees.

Now the sun casts shadows on my wall,
There's a prayer on every stone and tree,
I hear the cock crow a reminder,
The mountains of the Pyrenees

And my heart is lost in dreaming
Of the days I've been a rover
With the thought of being free
On the mountains of the Pyrenees.

DEDICATION & ACKNOWLEDGEMENTS

This book is dedicated to the quiet forces that have shaped my soul, and to the hands—both visible and invisible—that guided my pen.

To my family and friends: thank you to those who walked beside me, those whose necessary absence forced me into the stillness of my own company, and those whose quiet guidance in everyday life steadily anchored my spirit. Your influence is woven into every page. I hold a profound gratitude for those who have suffered much in this life, teaching me the deepest lessons of resilience, grace, and the human spirit.

And finally, to those who are no longer on this earth: though you have crossed the river ahead of me, your presence remains absolute. In these latter years of my life, whenever I stoop to consider you, your memory casts a long, brilliant light upon my path. You are gone from this world, yet you live on in the twilight before my moon rises, profoundly shaping the man, the songwriter, and the author I am today.

Thank you for being my ladder to the light.

EPILOGUE

When the Road Becomes the River.

In my younger years, in a search for meaning, I once traced a river from its source to the ocean.
Along the way, I recognised the many states of its maturity: from the fast-flowing rapids of youth to the turbulent waters of mid-life. And as the afternoon of life dawned on me, like a river moving at a slow pace—having the time to be a mirror image of the sky—I began to realise how much I had become like that river. Those whom I love, or still love, have moved on, just as old friends do.
The learning curve is exactly as Carl Jung suggested: we ought not to live the afternoon of our lives as we have lived the morning of our lives. We come to realise that the soul in its aloneness has to keep its own company. The things we buried in the past belong to the shadow self, which we must find the courage to face. We have to savour the shadow, for it holds a darkness that is in need of the light. If dealt with effectively, it must be scanned, allowing us to find peace within ourselves without clinging to another.
In doing this, we can help become a gateway to the light for others—not in the ways of the world, but in the ways of the spirit.

So, I recognise that my books and songs are, and always have been, a ladder to the light for me. Now, they also offer an opportunity for you. My aim is to encourage readers drawn to the spiritual essence in many of my books to join me in communion through my caminoway.com.au website, podcast link, and upcoming Zoom meetings on a regular basis—fostering mutual progress on our journey to the heart —the God within each of us. Together, we can build a community of like-minded individuals supporting each other and those in greater need toward the light. Keep an eye on the website for the podcast link and further announcements.

In summary, the flow of my books and songs mainly follows the spiritual steps that brought me to where I am now, like a spiritual person on a slow-moving stream. For it is in the twilight, before the moon rises, I once again see midday—for as the saying goes, *at midnight noon is born*—that I am aware of the new birth of creativity opening to me in this stillness. As I close this book, I await a message from the Maker, patiently waiting for the next step in my destiny.

Doug McPhillips

About The Author

Doug McPhillips, poet, singer, songwriter, and author, commenced his journey of discovery over a decade ago after life-changing experiences. The many tracks he traversed across the Northern Hemisphere and down under in Australia and New Zealand have led to the content of this novel.

Doug has written many novels, an autobiography, two books of poetry, and a travel guide. He has recorded and sung songs related to this work, featuring melody. Doug divides his time between work, family, friends, and those seeking guidance in following their heart's desires.

Publisher.
IngramSpark Publishing
1 La Verge TN37086
Nashville Tennessee.

Printed in Australia
Lightning Source
76 Discovery Road South
Scoresby, Victoria. 3179

www.ingramcontent.com/pod-product-compliance
Lightning Source LLC
LaVergne TN
LVHW050937210926
848482LV00013B/642